ADVENTURES OF A BOOKCOLLECTOR

This book is dedicated
to the memory of
Bernard Stone (1920–2005)

Philip Murray

Adventures of a Bookcollector

with an Introduction by

Dermot Healy

CURRACH PRESS

First published in 2011 by
CURRACH PRESS
55A Spruce Avenue, Stillorgan Industrial Park,
Blackrock, Co Dublin

Cover by Barrie Cooke
Origination by Currach Press
Printed in Ireland by Gemini International, Dublin

ISBN 978 1 85607 733 0

Contents

Bibliophiles are Gastronomes,
Gourmets, Gourmandes, Epicures.
Holbrook Jackson 1950

A Good Book is the best of Friends,
The same today and Forever.
Martin Tupper 1810–1889

It has been said that when man
Needs Company, a book is his best
Friend ; When in doubt, a book is
His advisor ; When in damp spirits,
A book is his comforter ; and when
A man is bored, a book is his
Best recreation ; Books are the lifeblood of Humankind.
Holbrook Jackson 1950

A good book is the precious life-blood of a master spirit,
Embalmed and treasured up on purpose to a life beyond life.
Milton: Areopagitica.

Introduction

Years ago when I was living in Brixton there was a loud knock on the door and out on the step was the postman with a special delivery of a copy of *Soft Day, a Miscellany of Contemporary Irish Writing,* edited in 1980 by Sean Golden and Peter Fallon. It was accompanied by a letter from a certain Doctor Phil Murray, asking me to sign my contribution, and also monies for a postal return.

When I opened the book I found that nearly all of the 33 contributions by the other writers had been signed, including Sam Beckett and Liam O'Flaherty and Seamus Heaney, and I was amazed that this gentleman would take a chance in sending off such a valuable document to a stranger he had never met, but I admired his pluck, so I think I signed it that very morning and posted it on before noon to the address in Sligo.

And so over the years this amazing trust Phil Murray has in sending letters and manuals and return postage to writers living all over the world has earned him a great collection; but it also came from personal contacts, as he headed off on long journeys to meet a writer living at a certain destination, or just passing through on tour. And then there is the host of literary festivals, book launches and readings he has attended for signatures over the last 40 years.

Adventures of a Bookcollector is a wonderful account of all these contacts he made during that time, but it also demonstrates his love of literature – throughout the book poems by various poets are inserted – and his love of those involved in the book-collecting trade, from Des Kenny to Jim O Halloran. His account of the famous bookshop owner Bernard Stone is masterly, and here I can pop in another anecdote of my own. Philip writes of the first time he browsed Stone's Floral Street shop – one of Bernard's bookshops – and that he had an uneasy feeling that 'I was being stared at by a bespectacled gentleman wearing a full tweed suit. It was as if he was waiting for me to put a book in my pocket and run, when he would raise the alarm. The gentleman in question turned out to be a wax effigy of Sigmund Freud. It was absolutely lifelike.'

Years later, I was launching a novel in Bernard's bookshop, the wine was starting to flow, the gang were gathering, and suddenly I saw an old mate of mine enter and stand – to the left inside the open door – in front of the figure of the old man offering him his invitation, and telling him how he was an old friend of mine. Can you hear me, sir, he said and he tapped him on the shoulder. Then he stood waiting for the nod to enter. When I approached him and told him he was talking to a waxwork, he looked at the Freud in disbelief, and shook his head.

Bernard Stone's personality comes alive in *Adventures of a Bookcollector* in a rare and fantastic trip through literature, Bloody Marys, bookshops, launches in London, trips to Sligo and into Connolly's pub, and then out to The Moorings restaurant in Rosses Point. Then the story moves on to the almost complete collection of the work of Seamus Heaney – in various languages – that Philip has put together. That enterprise has turned into a lifetime's occupation because of his love for the poet's verse. We travel through magazines, journals, embassies and on the way meet David Hammond, Michael Longley and Derek Mahon, Field Day and Gallery Press.

Phil's writing instils a world of wide, intimate encounters with a host of authors and books in a unique fashion. It all began in the sixties when he found himself looking at the book shelves in Kenny's bookshop in Galway, but the real book collecting started when he moved to Australia – where Phil lived for a time and met his future wife Vivien – when he began collecting the work of the Nobel Prize winner Patrick White. This was the first collection he put together and as he did so he gives a great account of scouting through the secondhand bookshops of Sydney.

On returning to Ireland he learns the true meaning of first editions from Des Kenny, encounters various traps in the trade, then heads off into a lifetime obsession. On the way we meet many souls from the past: John McGahern, Bruce Chatwin,

Spike Milligan, Benedict Kiely, Graham Greene, Richard Harris, Charlie Haughey, Kingsley Amis, Arthur Miller, the list goes on and on, and all of these meetings or exchanges of letters and books contain great anecdotes, and amongst them is a heart-breaking account of Francis Stuart and his cat. His correspondence with Lawrence Ferlinghetti – author of *A Coney Island of the Mind* – led to a lasting friendship, and with Phillip's help, the poet came and gave a tremendous reading in Sligo and visited the original Coney Island.

These encounters are rendered in meticulous prose, and you keep turning the pages to see who you will meet next; and then finally comes the publication of *The Whoseday Book* in 1999 which included the work of 366 Irish writers and artists and politicians. And again the doctor sets out on an intrepid journey to capture the signatures.

It was a massive undertaking that led him in every direction, out to islands, political gatherings, painters' studios, and into pop concerts.

Finally, when you have finished the book, it's the warm and generous personality of its brave author that emerges. Doctor Phil Murray has produced a rare and vivid memoir of literature, authors and book collecting. The old secondhand bookshops, now dwindling, have found a great friend.

After the launch of *Adventures of a Bookcollector* he can sign a copy of the first edition to himself for this book is another valuable publication that can be rightly added to his treasures.

Dermot Healy
9 September 2010

Prologue

Book collectors are attracted to book collecting for many reasons, among them the enjoyment or fun of the search, the love of the book as an object and the economic possibilities. Often all these reasons coexist to varying degrees. The thrill of the chase is for me the most important by far. Book collecting is something I drifted into. I never said to myself 'I am going to be a book collector.' Collecting is in fact a grand passion of which it was once said that 'one is hardly aware of its presence before it has complete possession of him' (Eugene Field, 1896, *The Love Affairs of a Bibliomaniac,* chapter 4, New York: Charles Scribners Sons). I should stress that I am essentially a reader and only secondly a collector. I am very strict with myself and only collect what I will read and enjoy. I have read every book I have ever bought, many of them several times over.

In buying books I have mainly acted on my own judgement. Of course, in doing this I have made mistakes. I have also learnt that the essence of a book collection is that it should have individuality, as there is no virtue in collecting the same sets of books as are collected by many other people. It is still a great thrill for me to find a book that I have been trying to locate for years. Also, as well as buying books because I wanted to read them, I have always been fascinated by secondhand books and secondhand bookshops. Even when I didn't have the money to buy anything I could spend hours browsing and be in seventh heaven.

Herbert Faulkner West famously said 'Some collectors desire beetles, while others have divergent and decided propensities for empty bottles, full bottles ... silhouettes, tea caddies ... horse shoes, postage stamps, old coins, dead butterflies, guns, stuffed owls, stuffed animals, stuffed shirts, candlesticks, trademarks, first editions ... Although it is quite evident that collectors are not entirely "all there", I have always found them to be nice, harmless people, whom any of my readers could invite home without danger of being disinherited' (1936, *Modern Book Collecting for the Impecunious Author*, Boston: Little Brown). Many collectors are indeed harmless but it is interesting to note that bibliomania is the only form of collecting other than kleptomania that has a medical name attached to it. Sometimes, indeed, it is referred to as 'the gentlest of infirmities' or again as 'a gentle madness' (there is a book of that title by Nicholas Basbanes, 1995, New York: Henry Holt).

To non-collectors, book collectors may appear to be sentimental, illogical, selfish, romantic, extravagant, and sometimes capricious. As well as that, non-collectors look on money spent on books as money wasted, although they do not hesitate to spend lavishly on all sorts of trivialities themselves. The hobby has been around since ancient times: the early Greeks garnered rarities just as obsessively as today's collectors, and were just as interested in condition, scarcity and quality.

Some secondary causes of bibliomania are acquisitiveness, variety, and fashion. Apart from the occasional eccentric, though, the collectors I have met over the years have mostly been quite normal people. There are of course obsessives who suffer from an advanced form of the disease, who on purchasing a book put it away unread and immediately start hunting for the next one on their wants list. The saying 'Once a collector, always a collector' still holds.

The seed for the present book was sown by my good friend Des Kenny, of the Galway bookshop of the same name, when we met at a book launch in 2008. That evening we were talking about books and sport when out of the blue he suggested I should write an autobiography with special emphasis on book collecting – one that would be a personal recollection rather than an academic treatise. I am still surprised at the speed with which I said yes. The only writing I had published previously had been 15 or so medical/political articles for the *Irish Medical Times*, some travel articles, and a few literary pieces here and there. So I had no idea where to start but I felt an autobiography cum memoir might be within my compass.

Later that year I was on holiday with my wife Vivien in

Kalkan, south-east Turkey, planning to visit archaeological sites and relax on the beach with books. Instead I didn't open a single book but spent the entire time recalling and making notes about people and events relating to books, ending up with two notebooks filled with jottings. Being separated from the rest of my library forced me to get my thoughts together in a way that would never have happened at home. The structure of a book began to emerge. After that I carried a notebook everywhere I went and wrote down thoughts as they came to me, becoming genuinely excited about the project as time went by. I can only hope that readers will find the results interesting, perhaps even enjoyable.

CHAPTER ONE

Early Life, Reading and Collecting

I was born in Nenagh, a town of about 6,000 people in the centre of North Tipperary, in October 1940. I was the second of three boys and spent my first fourteen years in the town. The enormous changes that have taken place since then can be seen from a book of photographs published recently: *Moments in Time: A Picture History of Nenagh,* which contains the archive of a local amateur photographer as well as contributions from his friends (Dermot Treacy, *Nenagh Guardian,* 2007). Most of the photographs, taken in the second half of the 20th century, are of both local individuals and groups such as the dramatic society, the Gardaí and the Legion of Mary, together with school classes and excursions. Naturally there are photos of old hurling and rugby teams, in some of which I featured. The poverty then is plain to be seen from the clothing in the photos, though Nenagh was by no means the Limerick of *Angela's Ashes.* As children, though, we were blissfully unaware of the situation and life seemed wonderful.

The first books I can remember were the colouring books given to us by our parents for our birthdays and at Christmas time. I can't remember the titles of these books but they were probably the same ones as everyone else had at the time.

Both parents were readers and we were encouraged to read too. Very soon we were devouring fairy tales such as *Jack and the Bean Stalk, The Tale of Peter Rabbit, The Story of Three Bears, Goldilocks and the Three Bears, Snow White and the Seven Dwarfs,* and many others. Bedtime reading was the norm, and if a favourite aunt or uncle arrived in the house at this time it was a great treat to have them read to us.

The first comic I brought home had been lent to me by a school friend and it was carefully vetted by my mother in case I was falling under a bad influence. These publications came from the pagan country across the water, so in the opinion of our elders couldn't be good or wholesome. The many comics that did the rounds included *Beano, Dandy, Hotspur, Rover, Wizard, Adventure Comics* and *Eagle,* all of which were published weekly in England. Most of these haven't stood the test of time, mainly because they were thumbed by so many grubby fingers, but occasionally a batch appears at Sotheby's or some such English auction house and realises thousands of pounds. They had wonderful eccentric characters such as Dennis the Menace, Lord Snooty, Roger the Dodger, the Bash Street Kids, Biffo (not our man!), Jonah, Minnie the Minx, and many, many others. The comic annuals which appeared at Christmas time were more expensive but were of a sturdier format. The *Boy's Own Annual* was the best known of these and every self-respecting schoolboy had a copy. These publications were tame in comparison to today's offerings.

Cassell's *Book of Knowledge* made an even bigger impression on us than the comics did. This eight-volume classic encyclopaedia was first published in 1930 and contained everything an inquisitive young boy would want to know, including pages of interesting photographs. The books themselves were large and covered in blue hardboard that fortunately made them very sturdy. Apart from the many times the three of us thumbed through them, they proved useful foundations for a cowboy fort when we were confined to the house on a wet Saturday. Sadly, these books have not survived, and I am sure that to look through them now would be a serious trip down memory lane.

Other books were obtained by swopping with other boys in the street. Soon I was reading Richard Crompton's *Just William* and *William the Detective* as well as the other titles in the series. Mark Twain and Edgar Burroughs were hugely popular, and cowboy books, particularly those by Zane Grey, were devoured too. The only title of Grey's that I can remember is *The Lone Star Ranger*. After reading cowboy books we went around the street for days afterwards with toy guns and holsters, playing out the scenes from the books.

My mother, like all Irish mothers at the time, was deeply religious and a daily Mass-goer. She subscribed to various Irish religious magazines which were published by missionary orders whose purpose was to raise money for the order and foster vocations. These magazines appeared monthly and were left discreetly on the kitchen table, no doubt to counteract the influence of comics. The only two such magazines that I can remember were *The Far East* and *The Messenger*, but we seldom opened them. They may still be published but I haven't seen one for years.

Censorship was rigorous in Ireland at the time and this applied not only to children's books but also to adult reading material. It is hard to believe now how many of our great writers had books banned, but in a contrary sort of way this notoriety later worked in their favour. Apart from state censorship, the Catholic Church ruled with a rod of iron, and it wasn't uncommon for the parish priest to denounce a particular book from the pulpit at Sunday Mass. As often as not, this tirade had the reverse effect to what was intended and the sales of the book increased dramatically during the following weeks. As far back as 1892 the Anglo-Irish writer Rebecca West denounced the practice of banning books, saying 'God forbid that any book should be banned. The practice is as indefensible as infanticide" ('The Tosh Horse', in *The Strange Necessity*).

Censorship didn't keep *Lady Chatterley's Lover* out of the country and somehow a copy reached Nenagh. That copy was almost certainly brought in from England by an older schoolmate who had opted out of school early and gone across the water to make his fortune. Just as with comics, *Lady Chatterley* was passed around the school yard but under no circumstances would it be brought home. The salacious bits were well marked. Occasional copies of the adult monthly magazines *Men Only* and *Tit-Bits* also appeared in the school yard. For most of us it was the first time we saw a picture of bare bosoms, particularly for those like the Murray boys who had no sisters.

My father read *The Irish Independent* every day and *The Irish Times* once a week, primarily to read 'Cruiskeen Lawn' by Myles Na Gopaleen, aka Flann O'Brien (Brian O'Nolan). That was when I first saw this great writer's name and read some of his articles. My father was an avid reader of detective stories, his favourite authors being Agatha Christie and Peter Cheyney. He also read everything by Raymond Chandler, Edgar Wallace and

Edgar Allan Poe, and he began passing on some of these books to us as we got older. His bookshelves were in the front parlour (the 'good room'), and as well as detective books by the above authors, I remember that the mixed selection included *Guerilla Days in Ireland* by Tom Barry, *How Green was my Valley* by Richard Llewellyn, and *Valley of the Squinting Windows* by Brinsley MacNamara. I read most of these when I was old enough and still have some of them.

My mother was also a reader, but like all mothers had less time to indulge herself. Her favourite authors were A. J. Cronin, Canon Sheehan, Maurice Walsh and Walter Macken, all of whom I would now call safe authors. I remember reading *Green Rushes* by Maurice Walsh, *My New Curate* by Canon Sheehan, *The Stars Look Down* by A. J. Cronin and *Rain on the Wind* by Walter Macken. These and other books by these authors were widely read at the time and I have a clear memory of my mother's copies stacked on a kitchen shelf. Books like this are rarely read nowadays, even though some are well worth the effort. They have simply gone out of fashion.

The *Hornblower* series by C. S. Forester and the *Biggles* series by W. E. Johns were hugely popular and I read and reread all of them. I also developed an interest in Dickens, all of whose books were available in the local library. At this stage of my life the books that made the most significant impression on me, however, were John Steinbeck's *Of Mice and Men* and *Cannery Row*, as well as J. D. Salinger's *Catcher in the Rye*. They were the first adult books that I read and they have stood the test of time. I have reread them many times.

As a family we were frequent users of the local library. Every book that was brought home got the usual inspection from my mother — not that she had anything to worry about, as every title had already been well vetted by the powers that be. Unlike the libraries of today, the stock was limited and there was no such thing as a travelling library. Of course, the number of books being published then was a drop in the ocean compared to the glut in today's market, on every subject under the sun.

Shops that sold only books, whether new or secondhand, were a rarity except in the main cities, but an occasional second-hand furniture store or junk shop carried a few shelves of well worn books. Nenagh had two newspaper shops that also sold some new paperbacks, mainly cowboy, detective or love stories. The monthly publications *The Reader's Digest* and *The Irish Digest* were to be found in most houses and were read by adults and children alike. It was a prudish society, though, and the *Farmers Journal* was probably the most risqué magazine on the shelves. It was unusual to see anyone with a hardback book as they were both rare and expensive compared to paperbacks.

In houses where people read, there were always a few shelves of paperbacks, mostly detective stories but with a few classics and religious books in the form of lives of the saints. Nobody I knew collected books in a formal way and the only houses that contained large collections were those of the gentry and the parish priest. Among the gentry many fine libraries were handed down from generation to generation, while the local Catholic presbytery would have one or two mahogany bookcases containing mostly hardback books of historical, topographical or religious interest and an assortment of novels and poetry. A lot of these would have been donated by grateful parishioners over the years, for services rendered. When the priest moved to another parish the books tended to be left behind for the new incumbent and in this way quite large collections were built up. Even today when a parish priest's library comes up for auction it generates great interest in the trade, as often there are rare and expensive books to be found.

For my secondary school education, I spent one year at the Christian Brothers school in Nenagh and the next five at the Cistercian College, Roscrea. Both the Intermediate Certificate and the Leaving Certificate curriculums included poetry and this was my first contact with the medium. I hated it with a passion and have no recollection of any of the poems we studied for either exam. For some reason poetry seemed meaningless to me. I couldn't make any sense of it and I certainly didn't see the beauty in it. In both schools we were encouraged to read in our free time, but the selection in their libraries was fairly limited and I read little, partly because I was becoming heavily involved in sport.

Like a lot of young men of my time, I entered a seminary when I left Cistercian College in the late fifties. The order I joined was the Columban Fathers, a missionary order based in Navan, Co Meath, whose newly ordained priests were sent to either South America or South-East Asia. Apart from studying philosophy and theology we were given a broad education in literature and the sciences. A few of us seminarians commuted daily to University College Dublin to study for a BA. During my two years in Navan we had a wonderful English teacher who was passionate about the writings of Joseph Conrad. Despite this, Conrad never became a favourite of mine, although I read *Almayer's Folly, Heart of Darkness, Lord Jim* and *Nostromo* and now know that we were being pointed in the right direction as regards good literature.

Only a few students stayed the course to ordination, a trend that has continued unabated. After Navan my next port of call was University College Dublin from where I graduated with a BSc in mathematics, maths physics, physics, and chemistry, followed by a Higher Diploma in Education. My reading horizons were broadening and I was reading everything from Joyce to J. P. Donleavy, my favourite authors at the time being Hemingway, Graham Greene and Steinbeck. Browsing through my bookshelves recently I came across a bunch of about twenty-five books which are the remnants of my youthful reading. Needless to say, they were neither hardbacks nor first editions but instead were well-thumbed paperbacks. How they survived several house moves and lasted till now I have no idea, but I am reluctant to throw them out as they are a memento of a particular time in my life.

During those undergraduate years there was less time to read as there was a lot of socialising to be done and sport was taking over our lives. There was also the little matter of exams to occupy the mind. However, in Dublin I was able to experience real bookshops such as Hodges Figgis and Fred Hanna's for the first time. The city was also full of secondhand bookshops and the ones I frequented were Greene's in Nassau Street, Eugene Mallon's in Parliament Street, Enda Cunningham's shop Cathach Books in Duke Street, and quite a few on the quays, including Webb's. All of these have now gone out of business except Cathach Books. Some of the owners have retired while others such as Neville Figgis have relocated out of the city. As the British journalist India Knight said recently in the *Observer*, 'a world without bookshops is an inconceivably horrible thought.' Of course, we had little money to spend on such extravagances as books in those days and most of what we read was as a result of swopping with fellow students. My most abiding memory of those secondhand shops is the smell of old books that hit you as you went in.

While I was doing my HDipEd I taught mathematics and physics at Beneavin College in Glasnevin and I returned to my alma mater, Roscrea College, the following year to teach those subjects. Though I liked teaching, I couldn't see myself doing it for the rest of my life. So once again I changed direction careerwise and decided that I wanted to do medicine, with the idea of becoming a general practitioner. At the same time I changed university and headed west to University College Galway. The year was 1965 and Galway was then a small city with no more than 2000 students at the university. The Institutes of Technology hadn't yet arrived on the scene. Galway was, and still is, a very vibrant and cultural place, heavily involved in the arts, with the students complementing the local population.

We all worked during our summer holidays, but work in Ireland was difficult to come by, due to a general downturn in the economy. We usually had to go to either England or America to work mainly on building sites or in factories. Luckily for me, though, the silver mines just outside Nenagh reopened just as I was about to start medicine. The mines had been worked unsuccessfully for many years but had now been taken over by Mogul of Canada, which had a very productive ten years there. Mogul paid good wages that allowed me to put myself through my medical course without borrowing money. During the annual three and a half months of working underground I had little time to read, as I was also giving private tuition in maths and physics a few nights a week. My most famous pupil then was the well-known Irish language poet Nuala Ní Dhomhnaill, who was brought up in Nenagh and was later to say to me, very much tongue-in-cheek, 'I am what I am today because of you.' In 1991 her book *Feis* was published and she gave me a copy which she inscribed 'Do Philib – I gcuimhne mo chleachta leatsa fadó – Nuala Ní Dhomhnaill.' ('In memory of the lessons I had with you long ago.')

During my time in Galway I had the good fortune to meet Mrs Maureen Kenny and the Kenny family in their bookshop/ art gallery in High Street. The bookshop was for me then, and still is, a mecca, even though in the sixties I could only look at the shelves containing everything from humble paperbacks to rare leather-bound volumes. It was commonplace to see famous writers and artists browsing those shelves too, always in deep conversation with Mrs Kenny. The business had been started by Maureen and her husband Desmond in 1940 and I would imagine a lot of people thought them mad at the time. Since then it has become a Galway landmark, even though they have closed the original shop and moved to Liosban on the outskirts of the city. It is one of the finest book emporiums anywhere in the world, not just for its stock of books but also because of its knowledgeable staff, particularly concerning Irish literature. My early meeting was to be the start of a long friendship with the Kenny family. In later years I attended some great occasions in the shop, usually centred round a book launch or poetry reading. Even now I go to Kennys whenever I visit Galway, and my reasons are, as always, to browse the shelves of a great bookshop and to have the chat.

Back in the sixties and seventies it was common practice for newly qualified doctors to go abroad, particularly to America, Canada and England. They went for various reasons, some for experience, some for money, and some just to get out of Ireland, where things were pretty depressed. I had no desire to live in either England or North America so instead I chose to go to Australia. This was a landmark time for me, with my life as a student finally over. Some of my less charitable friends said 'and not before time', and I suppose they were right.

I chose to go to Australia for adventure as well as to pursue my medical career. In those days very few people from Ireland went there. My family and friends thought I would never return but I always intended to do so. Apart from furthering my education I realised I had the chance of a lifetime both to travel and experience a new culture. To become a fully-fledged general practitioner I had to devote six months postgraduate training to paediatrics and a further six months to obstetrics, and though I could accomplish all of this in most teaching hospitals in

Ireland, by going abroad I could have the best of both worlds. It would be a step into the unknown as I had neither family nor friends in Australia.

Sydney was my chosen destination and when I presented myself at the Australian embassy in Dublin to apply for a visa the official interviewing me asked if I was going as a migrant or travelling in a private capacity. He explained that if I went as a migrant I would have the choice of either flying direct from London or travelling by ship from Southampton. The entire fare would be ten pounds, irrespective of which way I travelled. The thought of sailing on a journey of four and a half weeks round the Cape was very exciting, and that's the option I chose. The ship was the *Australis*, of the Greek-owned Chandris Line, and when it set sail some months later there were two and a half thousand passengers on board and a crew of a couple of hundred Greek sailors.

Australia was a very easy environment to settle into and I felt very welcome in every walk of life. Before I left Ireland I had arranged to spend my paediatric six months at Wollongong hospital in the Illawarra region of New South Wales, followed by a six-month obstetric term at Crown Street Women's Hospital in Sydney's eastern suburbs. During my time in Crown Street I lived in the residents' quarters of the hospital and was able to walk everywhere and explore the city during my time off. It was here that I met my future wife, Vivien Kennedy, who was then working as a midwife at the hospital, having just returned from working abroad. Such is fate! She was born and brought up in Sydney, and with a name like Kennedy had to be of Irish extraction. She is in fact fifth generation Irish but, try as he might, her father failed to trace their roots when he visited Ireland some years later. The closest he got was that a forebear might have left from Wexford during the famine, but relevant records of the time were no longer available. We got married in Mosman on Sydney's North Shore the year after I arrived and continued to live and work in Sydney for some months before moving further afield.

Sydney is one of the great cities of the world and it was an exciting time to live in Australia. The Sydney Opera House had just been completed and the McMahon government of twenty-two years was about to fall and be replaced by Labour under the charismatic Gough Whitlam. Though I am not a city person, I took to Sydney and its people right away. Melbourne claims to be the more artistic and cultured city, and to this day there is a healthy rivalry between the two. When the powers that be couldn't decide between the two as the country's capital city the honour went to Canberra, which is without doubt one of the most soulless and boring places I have ever been in.

My reading habit started up again in Sydney and I soon discovered that there were nearly as many secondhand bookshops scattered throughout the city and its suburbs as there were in London. The shops I remember best were the Antique bookshop run by Peter Tinslay in McMahon's Point, the Cornstalk bookshop in Glebe, Haymes and Sons also in Glebe, Tyrell's bookshop in Crow's Nest, Louella Kerr in Paddington, and the first edition specialist Nicholas Pounder in Double Bay. The largest bookshop in Sydney, and probably in all of Australia, is Berkelouw Books, whose main shop is in Paddington but who also have an enormous bookbarn in Bendooley in the countryside not far from the city. The principal new bookshops in Sydney were Dymock's and Angus and Robertson, both of which I frequented. On my days off work I visited most of these shops and got to know some of the owners. One of life's great pleasures to me is browsing in bookshops and getting the smell of the books even if I don't buy anything. Unfortunately secondhand bookshops are in decline in most cities of the world, mainly because of high rents and the advent of the internet.

There was a surprising amount of Irish literature in the various shops, but naturally the main stock was Australian. Most of the books by Irish authors were quite cheap but I resisted the temptation to buy as I knew that I would have to transport them home to Ireland at some stage. With Australia's image of being the country of the great outdoors, I was pleasantly surprised to find such a culture of reading. My own interests lay in indigenous authors and a friend recommended a series of Australian classics which had been just republished by Lloyd O'Neill. This became my first venture into Australian literature. There were twelve books in the series, the best known being Frank Hardy's *Power Without Glory*, Marcus Clarke's *For the Term of His Natural*

Life and Robert Bolderwood's *Robbery Under Arms*. They were indeed classics, well written and by authors rarely heard of in the northern hemisphere. They sold for three Australian dollars each and were the first hardback books I ever bought. They gave me a great insight into early Australian life and culture, and many had an Irish slant to them. It is thirty-five years since I first read them, and having re-read them recently I have a greater appreciation of them, probably because of my long association with Australia. I bought all twelve of the series and eventually brought them back to Ireland. The three mentioned above deserve to be on everyone's bookshelves.

Though I seldom read history, I was interested in learning about my new country so I next read Manning Clark's *A History of Australia*, which is regarded as the definitive history of the country. Then I turned to Henry Lawson's *Collected Works*. He is regarded by many as Australia's greatest and best known writer internationally and there is hardly an Australian anthology of literature that doesn't contain a contribution by him. It was said that 'What Burns is to a Scotsman, and Kipling to an Englishman, Lawson is to an Australian – the voice of his people.' He was a master storyteller, writing about bush life, the outback and adventure. The books I liked best were *While the Billy Boils, Joe Wilson's Mates, Send Round the Hat*, and *The Romance of the Swag*. These titles couldn't have originated anywhere but Australia.

Before my arrival the only Australian writer I had heard of, but never actually read, was Patrick White. When he later won the Nobel Prize he was described by the Royal Swedish Academy as the writer who 'for the first time has given the continent of Australia an authentic voice that carries across the world'. The first of his books that I read was *The Tree of Man*, followed by *Voss, The Aunt's Story, The Living and the Dead* and *The Vivisector*. He was a magnificent writer and to this day his books leave a big impression on me. He wrote twelve novels as well as four collections of short stories, two plays and occasional poems. His books were available everywhere, apart from his first novel, *Happy Valley*, which was extremely rare and valuable. Apparently only two thousand copies had been published and as it was poorly reviewed at the time there was a great scarcity of copies later on.

Over the next few years I managed to buy secondhand copies of all White's books apart from *Happy Valley*, and I also set about getting the various literary journals he had contributed to, which included *Australian Letters, Meanjin, Meanjin Quarterly, Overland, Australian Book Review, Australian Literary Studies, Quadrant* and *Southerly*. *The London Magazine* and *London Mercury* were the only two non-Australian journals that I could find to which he had contributed. Most of them I bought for two or three dollars each, and apart from the two English publications these would have been extremely difficult to track down in the northern hemisphere. For me it was a case of being in the right place at the right time.

White made his professional debut as a writer with his two early poems 'Meeting Again', and 'The Ploughman', which appeared in *London Mercury* in 1934. I bought a copy of this issue not because of the poetry but rather because it was White's first foray into print. I didn't actually read the two poems until years later but buying that copy of *London Mercury* was almost certainly the moment when I became a collector – by accident rather than by design. It was also the first complete author collection that I set about putting together. At this stage I didn't realise that I would get involved in other complete author collections. In fact, it seems that most collectors start out like this.

Years later, back in Ireland, I was browsing in a secondhand bookshop one Saturday morning when I spotted a copy of White's *Happy Valley*. To say that I was excited would be an understatement. After checking it several times I realised that it was the genuine article and bought it for the princely sum of ten old pennies. Naturally I was delighted with my find, but as I handed over my money I felt guilty about buying the book under false pretences, knowing that the shop owner was almost certainly unaware of this gem. At home I immediately started to read the book but when I reached page 162 I realised there was a fault: the next 40 pages were missing and in their place the preceding 40 pages appeared for a second time. The binding was perfect and hadn't been tampered with, and in every way it appeared to be a flawless copy. To make matters worse I couldn't finish reading the book and was later to find out that it was worthless. I felt hard done by after my major investment ...

Some time later I told Alan Lawson, Professor of English Literature at Queensland University, of my 'find'. He was regarded as the authority on White and was able to confirm that the book was indeed worthless. He very kindly photostatted the missing pages from his own copy and sent them to me so that I could at least read the text. It was an interesting learning experience. I have never come across this sort of thing again, nor have I ever seen another copy of *Happy Valley*. It would be fascinating to know how many other White devotees had bought this copy from its publication in 1939 to the time I acquired it.

Something that is not well known about White is that in 1935, when he was an undergraduate at King's College, Cambridge, he had a book of poems called *The Ploughman: and Other Poems* published by Beacon Press. Like many other authors who later became famous he wasn't pleased with the literary merits of his first book and was later to refer to it as 'embarrassing apprentice work'. When I wrote to ask him to sign my copy of his second book, *The Living and the Dead*, I asked him about *The Ploughman* and about *Happy Valley*. He was probably one of the first authors I wrote to and I did so with some trepidation, as I had heard that he was a difficult man and rarely replied to requests like mine. I felt very privileged when he answered my letter and followed up with a postcard in which he agreed to sign *The Living and the Dead*. The whole saga surrounding *The Ploughman* fascinated me. Only three hundred copies had been printed and he never allowed it to be reprinted during his lifetime, nor is it mentioned in his bibliography. Indeed, once when I was in Sydney the *Sydney Morning Herald* printed a front-page photograph of him publicly burning a copy of this book that he had just bought. It was then extremely rare and valuable and I can imagine that it is now even rarer, as he subsequently bought and burnt other copies before his death in 1990. A copy now would cost thousands of dollars. When White moved to his final home in Sydney's Centennial Park he had a small suitcase full of copies of *The Ploughman* and burnt them in a fire in the backyard. Unfortunately he added the manuscripts of *The Tree of Man* and *Voss* to the inferno by accident.

White is one of the best novelists I have read and he now holds a central place in the history of Australian literature,

N.S.W. 2021
10.xii.78

Dear Dr Murray,
Thank you for your letter of a long time ago. I'm sorry not to have answered before, but I've been up to my ears in work & illness.
My first novel Happy Valley hasn't been reprinted for various reasons. The book of poems is so embarrassing (it should not have been published) I wish it would go up in smoke as do any copies I can lay my hands on. So I can't give you permission to have a copy made.
Sorry if I disappoint you.
Yours sincerely,
Patrick White

though it was only after he won the Nobel Prize that he became popular as a writer, both at home and internationally, but he may well be the greatest modern writer about whom the least is known. Over the years he turned down the many doctorates he was offered, and even when he won the Nobel Prize he refused to travel to Stockholm. Instead he asked his friend Sidney Nolan, the internationally known painter, to accept the prize on his behalf. With the money he set up a fund for older Australian writers whom he felt had not received due recognition for their work. This shows that despite his reputation he was a man of principle. Apparently he preferred to talk about paintings rather than books and was happiest in the company of painters. I now know that he was a very private man, was known to have a savage temper, and didn't suffer fools lightly.

White both loved and hated Australia and was sometimes accused by the media of not producing 'the great Australian novel'. He was famous but was determined to keep fame at arm's length. He gave very few interviews and also refused to appear on either radio or television. He refused to teach even though he had many offers, and he had a great suspicion of academics and literary politics. He was not a recluse but rather an eccentric who saw himself as a sufferer, a theme that runs through all his books, especially *Voss*. It is reported that he read each volume of Manning Clark's *History of Australia* as it appeared, saying 'Interesting to see how we have remained the same pack of snarling mongrel dogs' – typical of the man. Later I felt how privileged I was that he had replied to my letter as well as signing my copy of *The Living and the Dead*. He was in his seventies at the time and reportedly in bad health, so I am sure the last thing he wanted was a letter like mine enquiring about *The Ploughman*, yet he obliged me. It was the quality of his writing that I was interested in rather than the man himself.

Of the many other Australian writers I read during my time in the country there were two whose work I particularly admired. The first was George Johnston, who wrote *Clear Straw for Nothing, A Cartload of Clay*, and *My Brother Jack*, his best known book, amongst others. The second writer was Thomas Kenneally, who comes from Sydney and is one of Australia's most prolific writers. He has published over thirty novels and books of non-fiction and is still writing. I bought and liked his early books best but *Schindler's Ark*, which won the Booker Prize in 1982 and later became the internationally acclaimed film *Schindler's List*, is undoubtedly his best-known book. He signed books for me, including *Schindler's Ark*, on several occasions.

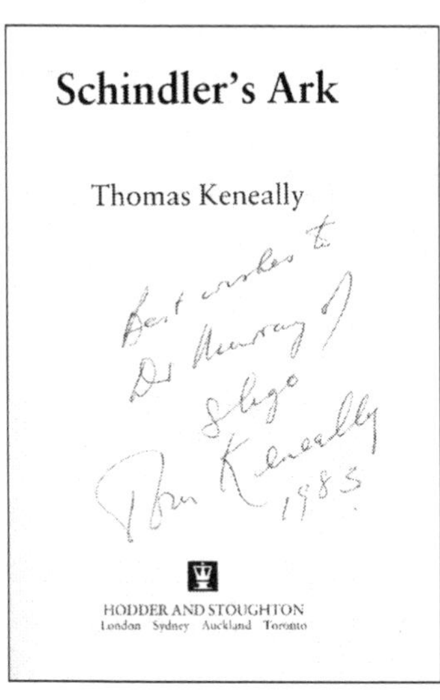
Schindler's Ark

Thomas Keneally

HODDER AND STOUGHTON
London Sydney Auckland Toronto

I like Australian literature and I continue to buy and read books by writers such as Peter Carey, David Malouf, Richard Flanagan and Tim Winton. Keneally and Carey have both won the Booker Prize and lifted the status of Australian writing internationally.

After my six-month terms at Wollongong Hospital and Crown Street Women's Hospital I started doing general practice locums in Sydney. The wanderlust was still with me, however, and as my medical degree was virtually a passport to travel I decided to work outside Sydney and see the country. One job was for two weeks in Sarina, a small town on the Queensland coast off the Great Barrier Reef. Another job for a similar length of time was in Narromine, on the Macquarie river in New South Wales. Needless to say there were no bookshops in either town.

A six-month locum then came up in Hobart and we decided to take up the offer. Vivien worked in a local hospital and we were provided with an apartment and a car. Tasmania is a backwater of sorts where a lot of people, particularly from Sydney and Melbourne, go to escape the rat race. Hobart itself is a lovely old-world city, very English in many ways. In those days it was full of bookshops but I am sure that, like everywhere else, most have now disappeared.

After the six-month locum was up we returned to Sydney for a few weeks before setting off for Ireland. By this stage I had acquired so many books that, with Vivien's collection, they filled four tea chests. Fortunately I had a rugby friend, Carl Phillips, who worked with one of the main shipping lines and arranged to have the lot transported all the way to Nenagh for a very small sum — that's what friends are for, isn't it?

CHAPTER TWO

The Odyssey Continues

On our return from Australia I found a job in Sligo, where we have lived ever since. The Irish climate with its long dark evenings lends itself to reading so I began to browse the bookshops and stock up once again. It wasn't that easy for us to settle as Ireland was a desolate place in the seventies, with massive unemployment and with emigration the only answer for many. Today's financial climate is a stark reminder of those days. Nobody had much money, including ourselves, and when we decided to put down roots in Sligo and enter the housing market we were refused mortgage facilities in one bank after another. It was soul destroying until finally a friendly bank manager took pity on us, when we felt privileged to be granted a mortgage at 17.5%.

My first foray into the world of books after returning was to buy a few sets of old classics published by Heron Books in England. These were being advertised in *The Sunday Times* and I acquired sets of John Steinbeck, Charles Dickens, Jane Austen, Winston Churchill's *The Second World War*, and the Russian classics. They were obviously not collectors' items but were well produced and reasonably priced. It was the first time I had read any Russian literature and the set I bought included the best-known works by Turgenev, Dostoyevski, Pushkin, Tolstoy, Gogol and Chekhov. Alexander Solzhenitsyn was the outstanding Russian writer alive at that time. He was a controversial figure and became world famous when he published his first book, *One Day in the Life of Ivan Denisovich*, in which he depicted his life in a prison camp. I toyed with the idea of writing to ask if he would sign my book but I thought that would be a bridge too far and desisted.

A few months after arriving in Ireland Vivien and I attended a friend's wedding in Castlebar and found that my friend Des

Kenny was a fellow guest. After sorting out the problems of the world we spent the rest of the day talking about books. When I told him what I was reading, and in particular about the Heron sets, he asked why I didn't buy books in first edition. The term *first edition* meant nothing to me at the time so he explained that buying a first edition cost the same as buying a fifth or tenth edition later on and that a best-selling book would be printed in many different editions. With few exceptions, though, the only version that holds its value is the first printing of a book. This was the first time value came into the picture and it made sense to me. From then on I tended to buy books in first edition whenever possible.

Des also educated me about such terms as manuscripts, proof copies, dust jackets, festschrifts, galley sheets, holographs, limited editions, broadsides, advance copies and other such words commonly used in the book world. The definition of a modern first edition is one published in the twentieth or twenty-first century, or its first appearance in print, however it is published. Such editions were once described as 'Those Immortal fledgelings of authorship, first editions of first books, still warm from the creative nest; first flights with the bloom of the author's love still upon them; first flights with the adorable clumsiness of all young things; copies which reflect the author's first hot, flushed stare of rapture when he looked upon what he had made and saw that it was good; such books will ever entrance the bookworm' (Holbrook Jackson, 1950, *The Anatomy of Bibliomania,* New York: Farrar Straus and Co). Non-book collectors sometimes wonder what is so special about modern first editions but collecting them may simply be an irrational form of human behaviour, like golf, for example.

Soon I was to learn that the modern first edition market was a growing one worldwide and that there were specialist book dealers who would be only too happy to add a name to their mailing list. Being on such a list entitled you to a minimum of four catalogues a year. Printing and postage costs mean that sending out such catalogues is not cheap, so even though there is no compulsion to buy, the dealer will take your name off his list unless an occasional purchase is made. Some people prefer not to buy from catalogues, because they often find that what they want has already been sold by the time they contact the dealer, leaving them disappointed. On the other hand, there are collectors who regard catalogues as indispensable, as the best ones contain much useful information and fine plates, with sometimes a relevant anecdote or an introduction by the bookseller. American and English dealers lead the field, with no more than a half a dozen in Ireland north and south. But now that the web and email have taken over, fewer catalogues are sent out.

As in other kinds of fine art collecting there are book specialists in every topic under the sun, including modern first editions. Specialist book magazines such as *Antiquarian Book, Rare Book Review, The Bookseller, Firsts* and many others contain all kinds of information relating to books, including the names, addresses and specialities of dealers all over the world. These publications can be valuable sources of information.

Modern first edition dealers and serious collectors have almost a fetish about whether or not a book has a dust jacket / dust wrapper. In their catalogues, dealers describe the condition of every book and its dust jacket in minute detail, pointing out whether it is a clean copy or not, whether it contains a blemish of any kind, and whether it includes a previous owner's name. Except under exceptional circumstances, such as extreme rarity or if the book is an association copy (a book or pamphlet that shows it had belonged to the author or someone closely associated with the author), most serious collectors will only buy a modern first edition if it is a clean copy with a dust jacket.

A first edition means the first impression of the first edition, so the earlier the better is the rule. Identifying the first impression of a first edition can be a nightmare, though, and like everyone else I have made mistakes. Obviously the author's own manuscript is the earliest and most desirable state of the book, but to acquire a manuscript is not an option in most cases. Most manuscripts end up in the author's archive and any that come on the market are expensive and as often as not are bought by libraries that specialise in the particular author and have a large holding of his or her books. The next best option is a proof copy, which represents an intermediate phase between what has been written and what is being prepared for general release. Despite the fact that proof copies are printed in small numbers – anywhere from 50 to 200 – they are not expensive. Publishing houses send such copies to critics and book trade buyers and unless the author has signed them they tend to cost the same as the hardback first edition. There are often textual differences between the proof copy and the final published book, which I think should mean that a proof copy would cost more.

The most notable mistake I made in this area happened in the early eighties when I bought a first English edition of Salman Rushdie's *Midnight's Children* shortly after publication for the published price of £6.95. Later that year it won the Booker Prize and the first edition was soon selling for hundreds of pounds. In early 1982, one year after its publication, I was browsing in a Dublin bookshop when I came across another copy, apparently also a first edition, still selling for the published price. Naturally I was delighted with my find. Before that time the words second impression, third impression, etc had been printed on the copyright page but a new coding system of numbers had recently been introduced worldwide, with the added complication that different publishers might apply the system in different ways. In particular the American and English coding systems often differed. When I checked my copy of *Midnight's Children* again I realised that it was the eleventh impression of the first edition and not even worth the published price.

Another area of confusion, and one where I made many mistakes, was in recognising whether an American or English edition was the true first edition. It took me a while to realise that American authors usually have their books published first in America, with the English edition published later that year, or sometimes years later. English and Irish authors of course usually have their books published first in this part of the world and later in America.

An extreme example of this problem occurred in 2009, when I bought the first English edition of Colum McCann's highly acclaimed *Let the Great World Spin* for the published price of €18.99. Shortly afterwards I received an American catalogue which had a copy of the first American edition on sale for $80.00. The dealer stated that this was the true first edition, as it had been published there ten weeks before the English edition. To complicate matters a subsequent catalogue had the Canadian first edition on sale for $120.00, stating that this was the true first edition as it was published two weeks before the American edition. To my mind this is splitting hairs, and it made me wonder how much time some dealers spend going through the various editions of books trying to spot significant differences so that they can offer them to their customers at inflated prices. I am happy to report that I am very content with my first English edition of *Let the Great World Spin*.

In the early seventies I bought a first English edition of James Dickey's *Deliverance* for £12.00. A short while later an American first edition was quoted in a catalogue at £150.00. When I made enquiries about this disparity in price it was explained to me that the American edition had been published in 1970, some months before the English edition. The price differential between the American and English copies of the same book may seem exorbitant, but it goes back to the old adage 'earlier is better', so the price was a true reflection of the market value.

Book club editions also gave me problems. These were usually hardback copies that looked just the same as the first edition of the book except that they had the words 'Book Club Edition' stamped clearly on the dust wrapper. What puzzled me was that they were extremely cheap and I couldn't figure out why until a dealer friend explained matters. In the late seventies I bought a first English edition of Harper Lee's only book, *To Kill a Mockingbird*, for £8.00. It went on to win the Pulitzer Prize and sell over thirty million copies worldwide so I really thought I had a bargain. Like the copy of *Deliverance*, a copy appeared in a catalogue soon afterwards for £180.00 and it was then that I realised my copy had 'Book Club Edition' stamped all over it, dramatically reducing its value.

Another trap I fell into on a few occasions was to buy ex-library copies of books. In the early eighties I was browsing in Foyle's bookshop on Charing Cross Road in London when I found a copy of the first English edition of Alan Sillitoe's *Saturday Night and Sunday Morning* for which I paid £4.00. When I started to read it at home I found the stamp of Renfrew County Library on the copyright page and twice more elsewhere in the book. Again a friend explained that I shouldn't buy ex-library books because they were not clean copies. Such books had lost their real value but more importantly it was likely that they had been stolen at some stage and sold on to an unsuspecting bookseller. I learnt some valuable lessons.

Prospective collectors like me find these things out the hard way but with luck the learning curve eventually runs in the right direction. It dawned on me quite early that not every book dealer necessarily knew everything about every book, and that ordinary collectors concentrating on a particular author would often know far more about that author than most general dealers, so bargains could often be found. And it is worth mentioning that more people are collectors than they realise, because most readers don't throw their books away when they finish them.

People collect for all sorts of reasons, including those like me who simply admire the author and want to read his or her books. Others collect because a book has a certain binding or plates of special interest, or because it has been published by a specialist press such as the Dolmen or Cuala Press. One dealer told me about a client who collected only the first book by certain authors. Another dealer told me of an American collector who bought a shelf of books from his shop because they were leather-bound and would look good in his bookcase back home. That collector had absolutely no interest in the content of the books. Then there are those who collect solely for investment, some of whom have unlimited funds and never read the books they buy, instead keeping them in strongrooms with their stocks and shares in the belief that such treasures will always sell at a premium. Some very wealthy collectors might commission a dealer to put together an instant library of modern or other literature without regard to cost. Others buy books as furniture to fill blank walls and in such cases booksellers are no more than interior decorators.

Some books of course attract enormous prices. Whenever one of the 100 signed copies of the 1922 limited edition of *Ulysses* comes to auction the price goes further up, as investors feel it is a banker. A copy of this limited edition was sold in London in 2009 for £275,000, the highest price on record for a twentieth century first edition. There are similar books that fetch ridiculous prices, not necessarily for their literary merit but because of their extreme scarcity or the fame or notoriety of the author. Ian Fleming's first four Bond books, *Casino Royale, Live and Let Die, Moonraker* and *Diamonds are Forever* were published in the fifties for 10s.6p each and now sell for £10,000 to £20,000 each, depending on their condition. Inscribed first editions of Fleming's books that mention James Bond in the inscription are even rarer and more expensive: a copy so inscribed was recently catalogued at €35,000. A mini-industry has sprung up around everything to do with James Bond, including soundtracks of the films, postcards and all sorts of memorabilia. The Corgi models of the cars that Bond drove, particularly his Aston Martins, are collectors' items and sell for hundreds of euro. The great popularity of the films must be part of the reason why the books became so valuable.

A more recent example of such extraordinary success is what happened with J. K. Rowling's books. Her first book, *Harry Potter and the Philosopher's Stone,* published in 1997, now sells for £25,000 in first edition, and a signed or inscribed copy would cost considerably more. The second and third books in the series, *Harry Potter and the Chamber of Secrets* and *Harry Potter and the Prisoner of Azkaban,* also sell for large sums in first edition, as the print runs were apparently small. The other four books in the series were published in large numbers and are not valuable unless they form part of a full set of seven. A dealer told me recently that he advises all his customers who have a first edition of any of the first three Potter books to put them in a safe and instead buy their child a new copy of whatever edition is currently available at the original price. The books in the safe may well provide the child with a down payment on a house at a later stage. The same sort of industry as with Bond is springing up around everything to do with Harry Potter.

Collecting translations into English is an area I know little about and have rarely heard discussed amongst the book fraternity. However I do collect two authors in translation: the Czech writer Milan Kundera, whose books were first translated into French and then into English, and Gabriel Garcia Marquez. The copies I have include both American and English first editions, with neither of course being the true first edition. The only other translations I have collected are single volumes and include *The Train was on Time* by Heinrich Boll, *The House of Spirits and Eva Luna* by Isobel Allende, *Maigret Takes the Waters* by Georges Simenon, *The Tin Drum* by Günter Grass, and Javier Marias's trilogy *Your Face Tomorrow*. The titles in Marias's trilogy (*Fever and Spear, Dance and Dream* and *Poison, Shadow and Farewell*) were published between 2005 and 2009, so I was able to buy them for the published price as they appeared, an added bonus being that they were already signed. Many regard them as modern day classics.

Nowadays I find myself reading more translations than before, mostly as a result of being told about them by friends. I usually borrow such books from the library but also buy some in paperback. My son Joe gave me a copy of Stieg Larsson's *The Girl with the Dragon Tattoo* early in 2009 and to say it was unputdownable would be an understatement. The other two books in the Millennium trilogy, *The Girl who Played with Fire* and *The Girl who Kicked the Hornet's Nest*, were published in English in 2009 and went to the top of every bestseller list in every English-speaking country. It is a rare for a sequel to be better than its predecessor but in this case the later books simply got better and better.

Larsson's trilogy must surely qualify as one of the greatest publishing successes of all time, with over forty million copies sold in thirty-five different countries at the time of writing. In the history of publishing, no Nobel Prize, Pulitzer Prize or Booker Prize winner has achieved the sort of overnight success gained by Larsson, who had never previously published a novel. For a translation to achieve this extraordinary success must create some sort of record in publishing terms. Larsson died at the age of fifty from a massive heart attack shortly after handing in the three manuscripts so there are obviously no signed copies of the books, though it has recently been disclosed that about ten copies have been signed by his translator Reg Keeland (Stephen T. Murray). One such copy recently sold for €5000, and this for a book just a year old. I think the dealer must have based his valuation on the fact that it was a first English translation and had the translator's signature. The dealer claimed that it was the next best thing to the author's signature, which is perhaps stretching things too far.

There is every chance that the main character in the three books, Lisbeth Salander, will become as well known internationally as James Bond and Harry Potter. Even though his success is posthumous, Larsson is now being recognised as one of the great talents of contemporary crime fiction, and Lisbeth Salander is being hailed as the most original character in crime fiction since Patricia Highsmith's Ripley in the early fifties. One thing is certain: the books have already earned a pot of gold for some people but it is sad that the man himself is not around to enjoy the fruits of his endeavours.

The other crime writer whose work I have been buying in paperback or borrowing from the library is Henning Mankell. He is best known for his Inspector Wallander novels but is also an occasional children's author and dramatist, and of course his television series is hugely popular. I was recently given a present of the first English edition of his most recent book, *Italian Shoes*, but Larsson's work puts Mankell in the shade. Of course, I am not able to comment on the standard of translation for these writers and the others mentioned here.

Naturally, demand is the main reason why books become valuable. When Peter Carey's *True History of the Kelly Gang* won the Booker Prize in 2001 copies of the first edition were suddenly selling for £150 whereas before the announcement was made they were selling for £20, which is what I paid for my copy. A fall in value may also happen, as it did with Louis de Bernières' *Captain Corelli's Mandolin*. When the film of this book flopped at the box office the price of a first edition dropped from £800 to £200. From an investment perspective, books and their authors can go in and out of fashion, so for those looking for profit there are no guarantees. It is a curious phenomenon but rarities do not always remain rarities. Even winning a major prize is not a guarantee of either literary or financial success, one of the best examples being John Galsworthy of *Forsyte Saga* fame: he won the Nobel Prize in 1932 but his books are hardly read or collected nowadays.

Most people who have a book collection, large or small, have no idea of its value and in the main don't dwell on it. It is no good buying books as a short-term investment but after enough time has passed any collection may include some books of value. There can be some disappointments, though. A friend once asked me to have a look at a collection of about 4000 books for which his aunt wanted some kind of estimate before she went to a dealer. The books had been acquired by her late husband over many years and she had high hopes about what she might get for them. The prospect of spending an afternoon going through this collection was very exciting but it was one of the saddest days of my life: I discovered that the books were almost worthless, apart from about six that might have been worth £200 in total. Their condition was uniformly shocking: nearly all of them were damp throughout and were fit only for the rubbish heap, as I had to tell her at the end of the day.

When you know what you want to collect it is usual to give a list of the books to a dealer, who will then give you first refusal when he finds one of them. Apart from this, one of the best ways I find of keeping up to date with interesting books and emerging authors is by way of newspaper reviews, particularly specialist papers like *The London Review of Books, The Times Literary Supplement*, and the Saturday review section in *The Irish Times*. Talking to fellow readers is another good way to keep up to date. Readers are only too happy to share their knowledge and will occasionally recommend a book or author you have never heard of before. When I like a book that has been recommended in this way I of course want to read other books by that author.

It is comforting to be able to report that during over thirty-five years of collecting I have found tremendous honesty in the trade. This is probably partly because only a quite small group of people is involved worldwide, so everyone tends to know everyone else, or at least to know of them. When ordering a book by letter, phone or email it is normal, once the dealer knows you, to pay after you receive the book. If the book is not as described verbally or in the printed catalogue it can be returned – hence the fastidiousness of the dealers' descriptions. I have only once come across a crooked dealer. That was about fifteen years ago when I received a catalogue from an English dealer whom I had never heard of before. At the time new dealers were springing up all over the place. When I browsed through the catalogue two things immediately struck me as odd. The first was that the terms stated that orders were to be accompanied by a cheque to cover the cost of the books ordered and the estimated postage cost. The second was the sheer quantity of rare books listed at knockdown prices. The whole thing was too good to be true and though I was sorely tempted I sat on the fence. Later I learnt that the gentleman in question was indeed bogus and had subsequently been arrested in London, though not before a lot of unsuspecting customers had sent their cheques to him. The disturbing thing was that this person had to be a book man to have the knowledge that he displayed in presenting and pricing the books. It was an embarrassment to the trade but a salutary lesson to collectors, making us realise that there are con men everywhere.

Forging authors' signatures, particularly if they are famous, can be a very lucrative business. I am not sure how prevalent it is at present but it is a practice that has gone on for centuries. Signatures supposedly by one well-known American author are currently being forged, so any signed copies of his that come on the market must be viewed with some suspicion. Where there is money to be made by fair means or foul we must remember the old dictum: *Caveat emptor*.

Sports books, mostly acquired as presents, make up part of my reading but any of these that might have been valuable have long since disappeared. My favourites in this category are books about rugby, dating back to early Lions tours, particularly those relating to my native Munster.

Before we came to live in Sligo I had read very little Irish literature but once there I began to read and collect writers from the Irish Literary Revival of the early twentieth century, including Seán O'Faoláin, Francis Stuart, Frank O'Connor, Seán O'Casey, Pádraic Colum, Liam O'Flaherty, Oliver St John Gogarty, James Stephens and Austin Clarke. The last three authors were the first poets I read on a voluntary basis, having first read their prose, and this was the beginning of my appreciation of the medium. I went on to buy and read *Wild Apples* and *An Offering of Swans* by Gogarty, *The Hill of Vision* and *Songs from the Clay* by Stephens, and *Pilgrimage and Other Poems* and *Flight to Africa* by Clarke. I appreciated the different styles of these three poets and liked what I was reading. Most of these books were not in great demand by the general public and could be found in any Dublin secondhand bookshop for little more than the price of a paperback, even though I was buying them in first edition.

Amongst these writers the one I had the highest regard for was Liam O'Flaherty, whom Anthony Burgess said was 'A major writer of fiction'. John Broderick said of him in *The Irish Times* that he was 'The finest novelist of his generation'. O'Flaherty became the second writer whose work I decided to collect in full. In all, he wrote sixteen novels, with *The Informer* and *Famine* being the best known and most widely read. Like Patrick White, O'Flaherty was also a master short-story writer, with thirteen collections published, the best known being *Spring Sowing*, and *The Tent*. In fact he was much more prolific than White, as he had 166 short stories published in all, though many of these appeared in literary journals such as *Cassell's Weekly, New Statesman, Lilliput, Spectator, Weekly Westminster, The Irish Statesman, Nation, Dublin Magazine, The Adelphi* and many others, most of these being either Irish or English publications. O'Flaherty also wrote biography, autobiography, book introductions, articles, book reviews, letters to the press and material in Irish. Some of his books were translated into a total of twenty different languages. Towards the end of his life he published *The Pedlar's Revenge* and *Wilderness*, two signed limited editions.

THE INFORMER

BY

LIAM O'FLAHERTY

Liam O'Flaherty

LONDON

JONATHAN CAPE LTD

Despite his huge output, most of his books and secondary material were easy to come by, though they still presented a serious challenge to a collector.

On one of my many book forays to Dublin during the eighties, I was browsing in Greene's bookshop in Nassau Street, always one of my favourite haunts and one where I found many treasures over the years. It mostly sold new books, including school books, but had a good secondhand section on the first floor. On this occasion I spotted six bound volumes of *Weekly Westminster* hidden away on a top shelf – I had obviously missed them on previous visits. When I got them down they had a thick coating of dust and had clearly not been disturbed for a very long time. They were dated from January 1924 to December 1926 inclusive. After seeing the dates, I knew immediately that they contained O'Flaherty material. In fact they contained a total of fourteen of his short stories. These were the first printings of all these stories and the only printing for some, as about half were never published in book form. The six volumes cost me all of fifteen shillings, but it was the fun of the finding rather than the low cost that made this purchase so exciting. I am sure the owner of the shop was wondering why I was buying this lot. He was probably glad to see the back of them, because as far as he was concerned they were just taking up valuable shelf space.

When I decided to ask O'Flaherty to sign my books, I wrote

to him care of Seamus Cashman of Wolfhound Press, as Cashman was republishing all his books at the time and was in many ways O'Flaherty's minder. Cashman arranged to have O'Flaherty sign some of my books and he and I have been close friends since the eighties. In 1996 the academic Dr A. A. Kelly edited *The Letters of Liam O'Flaherty*. About a year before this was published she wrote to me requesting copies of any letters I had received from him. She had obviously become aware through Seamus Cashman that I had corresponded with O'Flaherty. When the book was published she wrote 'The last two traceable letters are dated 24th March 1980, and 26th March 1981, both from Dublin, short notes addressed to Dr Philip Murray of Sligo, who collected O'Flaherty's work. The letters were probably written, certainly typed, by Kitty his partner, and Liam's signature is shaky.'

In his second letter to me O'Flaherty said, 'Once again I thank you for the two bottles of superb Bordeaux wine, delivered to me yesterday. It is very kind of you to add this wine to my cellar and I am most grateful. I am interested to hear of the material you have collected that does not appear in my bibliography and I look forward to hearing the details from Seamus Cashman. With thanks and best wishes, Sincerely, Liam O'Flaherty.'

Having taken the plunge into poetry, I now heard about an emerging poet named Seamus Heaney, a man of my own age, and I bought a first English edition of his book *North*. Published in 1975 this was his fourth book and was available in all bookshops for £2.95. His poetry immediately appealed to me and was very different from what little poetry I had read up to that time. When it was announced that Heaney was to read at the Yeats Summer School in Sligo that August I decided to go to what would be my first poetry reading ever. I had no idea whether it would appeal to me but in retrospect it was a wonderful experience, as I realised that having an author read his or her own work made it all the more accessible. After the reading at the Hawkswell Theatre he sat at a table in the foyer of the theatre signing books. Like many of the audience I joined the queue, met him for the first time and got my book signed.

Poetry was particularly strong in Northern Ireland at the time and I started to read and collect other Northern poets: like

Heaney, Michael Longley, Derek Mahon and John Montague were beginning to become household names. Even though their styles were different, they were and still are very talented poets. Around this time I joined both the Poetry Society of England and Poetry Ireland and am still a member of the latter. In this way I learnt more about poetry and poets. The Poetry Society issues a quarterly newsletter as well as four current books of poetry chosen by their committee. Their newsletter contains a section recommending various poets and their books, so I heard about international poets such as Ted Hughes, Carol Anne Duffy, Peter Porter, Lawrence Ferlinghetti, Wendy Cope, Douglas Dunn, Alan Ginsberg and Les Murray and was encouraged to buy and read their books. Poetry Ireland issues both a quarterly newssheet and an anthology entitled *Poetry Ireland Review*, which is a great forum for both established and up-and-coming poets, not just from Ireland but from all over the world. The review was launched in 1981, is grant-aided by the Arts Council of Ireland, and recently published its one hundredth issue. This is an astonishing achievement when one considers the number of such publications that have come and gone worldwide during this time. Ten years is the typical life-span of a literary magazine according to the poet Iain Hamilton.

Another aspect of my reading came when I first ventured into Anglo-Indian literature in the mid-seventies, when I bought and read Paul Scott's *Raj Quartet*. These books had a profound effect on me and made me want to read everything else in the same genre. The holiday I had had in India some years earlier was obviously an influence as I could almost smell the place when I read Scott's books. Since then I have read work by V. S. Naipaul, Shiva Naipaul, Vikram Seth, Rohinton Mistry, Arundhati Roy and of course Salman Rushdie. For some reason, these and many other Anglo-Indian writers all live in either England, America or Canada, which makes them relatively easy to contact.

My main interest in both reading and collecting centres around twentieth century literary fiction and poetry and I am always glad to hear about new authors. Everyone, of course, has his or her own particular tastes in reading. Some well-known and respected authors, among them Philip Roth and John

Updike, do nothing for me. I have had difficulty finishing their books so I don't collect either of them. *Ulysses* is a book that I attempted to read on four separate occasions before I finally made it to the end during a beach holiday when I was able to give it my undivided attention over a two-week period. It proved a great opener for conversation as while I was reading it several people who saw the title on the dust jacket said to me 'You must be either mad, or Irish, or both.' Having now read it through, I am none the wiser but have promised myself to give it another try.

Vivien is also a voracious reader and we quite often share books. I am delighted that the reading bug has been passed on to our children. None of them is a collector but like me none of them goes anywhere without a book. Fortunately we have a very good library in Sligo and are regular attenders. We didn't have a television set in our house until three years ago, and when we did decide to come into the twenty-first century we also bought a DVD player so that we could watch old films. Our reading habit has hardly been affected as the television set is in one of the children's bedrooms, so it is only when we really want to watch something that we leave the fireside and go upstairs. Our children must sometimes have felt deprived, growing up without television and having to listen to their school friends discuss the latest episode of *Neighbours*. The local postmaster used to send me an annual reminder pointing out that I hadn't paid the television licence. We got to know each other quite well as I had to phone to let him know that we didn't own a set. He must have thought us odd, to say the least.

In 1980 Wolfhound Press/Notre Dame published *Soft Day – A Miscellany of Contemporary Irish Writing*, jointly edited by Peter Fallon and Sean Golden. It featured the writing of thirty-six living Irish writers, presented in chronological order from Liam O'Flaherty, Francis Stuart and Samuel Beckett right down to Paul Muldoon, Harry Clifton and Edward Brazil. In the words of Sean Golden, 'This selection is quite deliberately a miscellany rather than an anthology. It does not attempt to establish canons of taste, or to collect the best of the work produced by contemporary Irish writers. Instead it samples what is being currently written in Ireland, or by Irish writers, providing a cross-section to be updated regularly, a showcase for work as it is produced, rather than a museum showcase. Our main difficulty in assembling this selection has been an abundance of suitable material.' Amongst the contributors were one Nobel Prize winner, Samuel Beckett, and one future winner, Seamus Heaney.

On one of the occasions that I sent my books to Liam O'Flaherty for his signature I enclosed my copy of *Soft Day* and he became the first to sign it. I then had the crazy idea of trying to get all the contributors to sign. I don't know why I embarked on such a mission but I like a challenge and I also felt it would be fun. Previously I hadn't been much of an autograph hunter and wasn't quite sure how to go about it.

Samuel Beckett was an author I had long wanted to write to, but I had kept saying to myself I shouldn't bother him. I knew he had the reputation of being a near-recluse but I knew little about him. I greatly admired his writing and was aware that he was one of the most influential playwrights of the post-war period. In 1981 I decided I had nothing to lose by writing to him care of Editions De Minuit, his Paris publisher. When I did this I said I would pay return postage on the parcel. He wrote back by return of post agreeing to sign and said 'Under no circumstances send return postage.' One of my prized possessions is the first English edition of *Waiting for Godot* so I sent it along with *Soft Day*. They were returned to me a week later duly inscribed. Over the following years, I wrote to him on four separate occasions and each time he not only inscribed others of his books

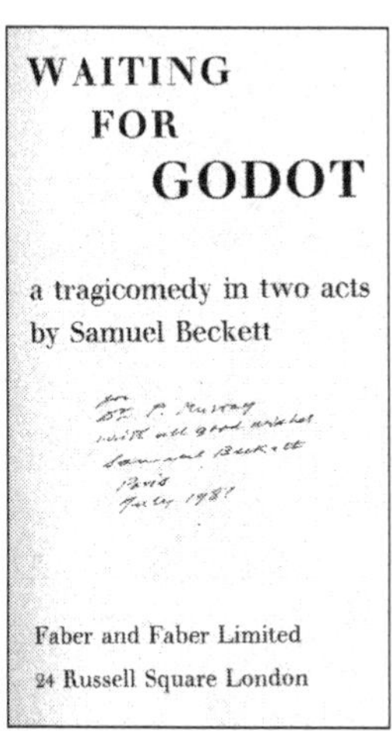
WAITING
FOR
GODOT

a tragicomedy in two acts
by Samuel Beckett

Faber and Faber Limited
24 Russell Square London

that I had bought but also insured them at his own expense before returning them. Some time later I was going to Paris for the biannual thrashing of the Irish rugby team by their French counterparts and considered contacting him with a view to meeting for a drink. But I was too shy and didn't want to interfere with his privacy, a decision I regret to this day.

Now that I had O'Flaherty's and Beckett's signatures in my copy of *Soft Day* I was encouraged to set about getting the rest. Most of the contributors lived in Ireland and were easy enough to contact. One well-known poet, who had better be nameless, thanked me for my offer of return postage and said 'Would you also stick in an English five pound note?' He didn't say what he wanted it for but I complied with his request. Another contributor replied, 'I am rather puzzled by your request, not having been asked to sign anything except cheques etc in the past. Or did I, methinks, renege on medical debts outstanding in the west long ago and have you eventually tracked me down?'

Another well-known poet wrote a long letter in reply to my request, saying that he would be happy to sign and expressing his thanks for my offer of return postage. I sent the book and enclosed relevant postage but then heard nothing more. After about a month I wrote to ask about the book as I was getting anxious that I might never see it again. He replied with extreme courtesy saying that his health wasn't great and that he had been very busy, but that he could be found in Slattery's pub in Rathmines any Friday evening between six and nine o'clock. I suspected that the return postage had long since been drunk. Shortly after this, Vivien was going to Dublin and was delegated to go to Slattery's in the hope of rescuing the book. When she went into Slattery's the barman informed her that the gentleman in question was in the adjacent snug with four friends. She introduced herself to them and bought a round of pints, after which the poet informed her that he hadn't yet got around to signing the book, so perhaps she should call again later. On her third such visit a month later, after the usual rounds of pints the poet's friends persuaded him to go to his nearby flat and get the book. He went off and returned with the book duly signed, but in his absence his friends had drunk his pint.

Over the next few years I took *Soft Day* to some of the authors and posted it to others. There were no further complications and all thirty-six contributors and the two editors signed for me. Sean Golden was the last to do so when I met him at the Yeats Summer School a few years ago. Whenever I meet any of the contributors now they ask if I managed to get everyone to sign. They are genuinely pleased to hear the outcome and all said they admired my stamina. This enterprise was the first of several such crazy notions, about which more later. The Odyssey goes on, even though nowadays I do more reading than collecting.

CHAPTER THREE

Bernard Stone, Guru

The next stage in my collecting life began when Bernard Stone – bookseller, publisher and writer – appeared on my horizon. Little did I know when I first met him in the seventies that he would become the single most important influence in my book-collecting life.

Bernard's four great passions in life were books, people (particularly book people), cigarettes and Bloody Marys, but I am not sure in what order. As a bookseller the most important thing he brought to the business was the fun element, and when he died in 2005 literary London lost one of its most endearing characters. He was described once as a sprightly tortoise with a touch of the mole about him. He spent most of his time doing you a favour or giving you a present. It is said that he spent more time talking about books than selling them. The American writer Timothy Steele wrote to me that 'He was clearly a remarkable individual. Let's hope he is not part of a vanishing species – the true bookman. In the United States, the publishing and selling of books is increasingly dominated by corporations and conglomerates, and these outfits tend to focus attention on blockbusters, and let such genres as poetry and literary fiction shift for themselves.'

Bernard Stone was born Barnett Finkelstein in London on 23 April 1920, the child of Jewish refugees from Odessa in the Ukraine. He had fifteen siblings, no formal education, was raised in Nottingham, and was known affectionately by his nephews and nieces as Uncle Bunny. He served for six years in the Royal West African Frontier Force, unlikely though this may have seemed to those who knew him later. At an early stage of his life, he found Nottingham too restrictive so he moved to London where, after some experience as a street trader, he set up a bookstall at poetry readings and similar happenings. It was at these get-togethers that he met the rising poets of the fifties, including Christopher Logue, Jeff Nuttall, Alan Brownjohn, Edward Lucie-Smith, Eric Mottram, Ted Hughes, Alan Sillitoe, Dannie Abse and Lawrence Durrell, who was to become one of his closest friends.

In the early sixties Bernard opened the first Turret Bookshop in Kensington Church Walk and the shop became the meeting place of the new generation of poets as well as some of the already famous. The Turret was one of the few places in London where their books could be bought.

Because of rising rents, Bernard moved to three other places in London during his lifetime. From Kensington Church Walk he went to 43 Floral Street in Covent Garden, then on to 42 Lamb's Conduit Street in Bloomsbury, and finally to Great Queen Street back in Covent Garden. Although he did so much for literature, particularly poetry, the Arts Council was never prepared to help with the costs involved. However, in spite of the changing addresses, Bernard knew that wherever he moved old friends would be sure to find him. One friend said that Bernard made sure of that by leaving a trail of rice crackers from door to door. To mark these moves, Hugo Williams wrote the following lines ('The Shelf Life of Bernard Stone', 1993).

To Bernard, On the Move Again

Which of us has got the strength
In this day and age
To up sticks
And start all over again
In a new location?

Obviously you have.
You seem to be signalling
With the usual welcoming
Paper cup
Of white wine.

Moving is supposed to be
Almost as bad
As divorce.

(They can be the same thing.)
I wouldn't know.

But it can't be as bad
When you aren't going
Very far
And you know very well
Everyone will follow you there.

Old faces in old places
Are always superior
To new faces in new places,
But old faces in new places
Might be even better.

Bernard's various premises were all decorated with portraits of famous poets of the past and hopeful poets of the future. There were postcards from all over the world, carpets on the floor, plants on tables strewn with books, and comfortable armchairs here and there. No other bookshop I have visited anywhere in the world has had the same style and ambience. A mutual friend once said that Bernard transformed every bookshop he presided over into a wine-stained club. In each of the four shops he leased, poetry was the house speciality. Some years ago Illtyd Harrington said in 'West End Extra' (*Camden New Journal*): 'His mother wanted him to follow the family tradition and become a cantor in the synagogue, but the religious faith was not for him. God, I think, forbade him – he is no singer.' Even though he wasn't a singer, he would occasionally break into his favourite song:

Another bride,
Another June,
Another sunny honeymoon.
Another season,
Another reason,
For making whoopee.

Bernard was also heard to sing to himself 'It had to be you, it had to be you' and he certainly made whoopee throughout his life.

Michael Horowitz said in 1974 that the Turret Bookshop was

'The merriest backwater at that time', and Bernard's friendly presence created a relaxed atmosphere for browsers. It was also described as 'A rendevous for poets, tosspots, literary genii, and aspiring writers.' It was said too that 'A visit to his shop on a Saturday afternoon or for an evening's poetry reading was a mixture of an audience with a mischievous pixie and a consistently kind Jewish mother.' One frequent attendee at these parties was Sir John Waller, who invariably turned up with a tough-looking semi-literate gay pick-up, whom he would introduce as 'a wonderful new poet'. Another regular was the novelist Alexander Trocchi, a drug-addicted hell-raiser. When you entered the shop you were exhorted to eat and drink. The wine flowed, with Bernard presiding over the occasion, a kindly Dickensian character. Yet another description was 'One of the true shops of character in Covent Garden (on his two sojourns there) and possibly in London – a mismatch between a social club, Aladdin's cave, and of course a very special bookshop with Bernard's personality oozing out of every corner.'

Bernard was a very good-humoured individual who brought a sense of joy to everything he did. As well as that he was extraordinarily generous, not just in dispensing drinks but in sharing his vast knowledge of books and giving advice. Perhaps his most endearing virtue was his tolerance. His advice was sound because he wasn't just trying to make money. He negotiated deals on behalf of writers, selling their manuscripts to collectors or American universities. He often discreetly paid an impoverished author an advance from his own pocket before a deal with a buyer had been agreed.

Bernard was not just a bookseller: he also wrote *A Day to Remember* and *Preparing Art for Painting* with co-authors. As a writer he was perhaps best known for the three classic children's books he wrote in collaboration with his friend the artist and cartoonist Ralph Steadman: *Emergency Mouse, Inspector Mouse* and *Quasimodo Mouse*. Another two books were produced with the illustrator Tony Ross: *The Charge of the Mouse Brigade* and *The Tale of Admiral Mouse*. *Emergency Mouse* was a bestseller. These books were written in the late seventies and early eighties and have become quite rare collectors' items. *Inspector Mouse* is of course Bernard himself in Ralph

Steadman's drawings. The books have lasted well and are still devoured by today's children. They are also the type of children's books that adults often keep for themselves. Yet Bernard never mentioned the success of *Inspector Mouse* to the poets who called to tell him of their neglected talents and to borrow his money.

Like 18th century booksellers Bernard made an occasional foray into publishing. The Turret Bookshop provided the base for this, with Café Books, which specialised in pamphlets by young poets, and Steam Press and Turret Press, both run in partnership with Edward Lucie-Smith and George Rapp. Bernard published many fine editions of such writers as Ted Hughes, Christopher Logue, John Heath-Stubbs, Louis Zukovsky, Bill Butler and Ruth Fainlight. Some notable publications were *Scenes from a Floating Life* by Henry Miller, *Twelve More Letters* by Dylan Thomas in an edition of one hundred and seventy copies; *Three Women, Wreath for a Burial* and *Uncollected Poems* by Sylvia Plath, and *The Threshold* by Ted Hughes in an edition of one hundred copies. The Turret Press also released some recordings, the most notable being *Ulysses Come Back* by Lawrence Durrell in a limited edition of ninety-nine copies in 1970. Bernard was also very supportive of emerging poets such as Adrian Mitchell and the Liverpool Poets Roger McGough,

Adrian Henri, and Brian Patten. Later Carol Anne Duffy and the Irish writers Matthew Sweeney and Desmond Hogan benefited too.

When a book was launched at the Turret Bookshop there was the inevitable party, with wine flowing freely. Some of these launches were paid for by the publisher but otherwise Bernard footed the bill. Dispensing largesse in this way often cost Bernard more than the subsequent takings in sales. Apart from the writers already mentioned, the roll-call of the famous who frequented the shop was like a league of nations. The list included Allen Ginsberg, William Burroughs, Seamus Heaney, Roger McGough, Lawrence Ferlinghetti, Adrian Henry, Stephen Spender, Gregory Corso, Adrian Mitchell, Dermot Healy, Alan Sillitoe, Fiona Pitt-Kethley, Ted Hughes, Derek Mahon, Harold Pinter, Benedict Kiely and many many others. When Allen Ginsberg visited in 1993 Bernard got him to inscribe a copy of *Empty Mirror* which he sent to me. There were other kinds of visitors too: on one occasion the actress Diana Dors came to browse, though Bernard never revealed whether she bought a book. He later told me that he didn't recover for a week after her visit, as he sighed for what might have been. In 1994 Benedict Kiely wrote: 'London for me meant Bernard Stone and books in plenty standing in display all around me, being quietly opened and wisely discussed. To this day when I encounter anyone on his or her way to London, I always say "But you must visit Bernard Stone." He takes precedence for me over the many wonders of this wonderful city' (*Book 'im*, 1994).

Each time the shop moved there was an all-day party to christen the new premises and help Bernard to settle in. The move from Lamb's Conduit Street to Great Queen Street was no different except that a barrel-organ was playing in the street outside, directly opposite the local Freemasons' lodge, and Ralph Steadman was playing on what he called his guitar. What the Freemasons and the passing public thought of the goings-on is anybody's guess. I suspect they were not amused. One of the tributes paid to Bernard that day was a poem written for the occasion by Adrian Mitchell, which he sang to the tune of Elvis Presley's 'King Creole' (*Camden New Journal* 13/5/93).

Ode to the King of Books
His daddy was a Russian, his mama was a Pole
He got ninety proof vodka in his soul.
He the king of books upon a tottery throne
And he goes by the name of Bernard Stone.
And he's gone gone gone.
Jeffrey Archer touched him for a loan.
Yes he's gone gone gone
Booksellin' Bernard Stone.

While the critics are oiling literature's hearse
He runs a nursery playgroup for British verse.
It's a place where the damned and the beautiful meet
Slap bang in the middle of Queen Street.
And he's gone gone gone
Happy as a barker with a bone.
He's gone gone gone
Booksellin' Bernard Stone.

Now Jeremy Reed has more flowing hair
But the women love Bernard like a teddy bear.
He's poetry in motion and he woos in rhyme
He may be Russian but he takes his time.
And he's gone gone gone
Older than the life of Titus Groan.
He's gone gone gone
Booksellin' Bernard Stone.

When it comes to book signings he is super-hip
Like Princess Di launching a battleship.
The wine keeps pouring to fill the void
Till you feel like that effigy of Sigmund Freud.
O he's gone gone gone
Open up a dozen Côtes du Rhone.
He's gone gone gone
Wine-swillin' Bernard Stone.

He sells you Ralph Steadman and if that ain't enough he
Sells you the collected works of Carol Ann Duffy.
He sells you Christopher Logue and if your hangover's deadly

A slightly stained secondhand Fiona Pitt-Kethley.
For he's gone gone gone
Lewis Carroll wants me on the phone.
Yes he's gone gone gone
Booksellin' Bernard Stone.

He doesn't come from remaindered stock,
Not Bernard the Stone but Bernard the Rock.
He's the poets' pal and he's the mouse's mate,
The King of Bohemia, Bernardo the Great.
And he's gone gone gone
Helper of the lost and the unknown.
Gone gone gone
Our beloved Bernard Stone.

My first contact with Bernard in the mid-seventies came after I saw an advertisement for the Turret Bookshop which stated that the shop carried a large stock of poetry, with particular emphasis on Irish literature. In fact it carried the largest stock of Irish literature, particularly poetry, of any bookshop in London. After writing and letting Bernard know what I was interested in, I made my first purchases when I bought some poetry journals by post.

Soon afterwards Vivien and I were on a short break in London and paid our initial visit to the Floral Street shop. We arrived at about half-past three on a Saturday afternoon to find the shop full of people in animated conversation, everyone with a glass of wine in hand. As I was browsing a shelf of books just inside the front door I had an uneasy feeling that I was being stared at by a bespectacled gentleman wearing a full tweed suit. It was as if he was waiting for me to put a book in my pocket and run, when he would raise the alarm. The gentleman in question turned out to be a wax effigy of Sigmund Freud. It was absolutely lifelike and had been made by Bernard's friend the sculptress Lynn Bamber. We learnt later that every time Bernard moved shop Sigmund came with him. When I had recovered from the shock of seeing Sigmund we introduced ourselves to Bernard and were immediately fortified with a glass of wine. It was to be the first of many such times spent with him. Unintentionally he instilled a great love of books in me, for which I am eternally grateful. The seed was obviously there but he fostered it as only he could.

During our conversation that first evening he informed me that he had never been to Ireland but had a great desire to visit the country. So I wasn't too surprised when he phoned a few months later to say he was coming over for a visit with Raymond Danowski, an American poetry collector who at the time was putting together an enormous collection of twentieth-century poetry. (The collection was later donated to Emory University library, Atlanta, when it was valued at two and a half million pounds. It contained letters and first editions of Samuel Beckett, W. H. Auden and Seamus Heaney, amongst others.) The visit to Ireland was to check out the main bookshops in Dublin, Belfast and Galway, with the express intention of buying Irish poetry for Raymond's collection. I invited them to come to lunch at our home in Sligo during their trip.

For Bernard it was the beginning of his love affair with the town and with Ireland. He became a complete hibernophile, visiting at least twice a year, always with a young lady in tow. (He adored women, and they him.) Before his visits he would phone to arrange a weekend that was mutually suitable and at the same time ask me to book two rooms in his name at the nearby Ballincar House Hotel. Bernard had spent most of his life in a small flat in the middle of London and it was in every sense a breath of fresh air for him to spend a weekend in the West of Ireland. After his first few visits he abandoned the bookshops of Dublin, Belfast and Galway and instead came directly to Sligo to make whoopee. Vivien would usually take him for a walk on the Hazlewood sculpture trail on the shores of Lough Gill, just a few miles from Sligo, which had a series of outdoor sculptures by Irish and international artists. While doing the circuit Bernard would sing away to himself, smoke cigarettes, try to shed his hangover, and admire the view.

He and his chosen partner for the weekend used to fly to Dublin and arrive at Sligo station on the Friday afternoon train, where I would collect them and bring them straight to Connolly's pub in the middle of the town beside the Garavogue river. For those of you who don't know this wonderful establishment I must describe it, because it will feature often in the rest of this book. Connolly's has now been a working pub for one hundred and twenty years and my friend Gerry Nicholson is the fourth generation member of his family to run it. It was originally a bar-cum-grocery, well known for its blends of tea as well as for bottling its own whiskey. The grocery end of the business went long ago, when supermarkets started to spring up everywhere. As well as having a Kilkenny flagstone floor, the pub has numerous snugs with timber and glass partitions and a recently installed pot-bellied stove. There isn't a bit of plastic or carpet to be seen anywhere. People from every walk of life drink in the pub, which is always a good sign of an establishment. Most importantly it serves a wonderful pint of Guinness. It is a favourite centre where people gather after local poetry readings, book launches, art exhibitions and sporting events. Many famous artists and writers, as well as sporting aficionados of every discipline, have passed through the pub's doors over the years.

On one of Bernard's visits he arrived with Martina Berne, a beautiful long-legged Dutch television presenter. When they came in to Connolly's that evening, the collective blood pressure of the male clientèle present was raised a few notches, much to Bernard's amusement. On most of his visits, though, he was accompanied by Lynn Bamber, the creator of the Sigmund Freud effigy. She is a highly regarded artist whose work includes limited editions of bronze heads of Seamus Heaney, Lawrence Durrell, Spike Milligan, Derek Mahon and Christopher Logue.

On one such visit Lynn, Vivien, Bernard and I went to The Moorings, his favourite restaurant in nearby Rosses Point. As he was entering the establishment he tripped and fell. The front of his head struck a concrete step and suddenly there was blood everywhere. As I helped him to his feet I saw he had a four-inch laceration on his forehead. A lady who was just leaving the restaurant became quite hysterical when she saw the blood oozing from the gaping wound and she started shouting 'Would someone please phone for a doctor?' When the owner of the restaurant arrived on the scene I could see he was possibly worried that a legal case might ensue. He was a friend of mine so I was able to reassure him that nothing would be further from Bernard's mind. I then put the 'patient' in my car and returned to my house to stitch him up. Bernard was of course short-sighted and would like to think that the fact that he tripped had nothing to do with the number of Bloody Marys he had consumed.

When we arrived at our house my younger daughter Jenny and a friend of hers opened the door and were horrified to see the state of Bernard, with his face and shirt covered in blood. He called the girls his Florence Nightingales and as I was stitching his scalp they each held one of his hands while he sang 'Tiptoe through the Tulips'. There was no need for me to administer a local anaesthetic: he was extremely relaxed and didn't feel a thing. While all this was going on, my son Joe arrived on the scene and was immediately dispatched to Bernard's hotel to ask for 'a clean shirt for Mr Stone'. With six stitches in his scalp and a clean white shirt on him Bernard was again ready to make whoopee. Back at the restaurant, he ordered a double Bloody Mary to compensate for the loss of blood, and so the night continued. The next day I wasn't sure whether he was concussed or hung over or a mixture of both. I never found out what he told his friends in London about how he had acquired the scar on his forehead. There was some talk later amongst the London litterati that he had been involved in a yachting accident in Sligo Bay. This was never verified to their satisfaction and there the matter rests. By the time Lynn and he left on the Monday morning all concerned knew that it had indeed been a long weekend.

Bernard fell in love with Connolly's and referred to it as 'his spiritual home'. As well as befriending the owner he got to know my other friends and many of the other locals. Regularly at about eight o clock on those Friday evenings he would sidle up to each woman in the place in turn – all five foot four inches of him, which would bring his head level with a certain part of the female anatomy – and then whisper 'Any chance of a bit of nooky?' If any of the rest of us had carried on in the same way we would have been sent packing, with a good wallop. But the ladies never said a cross word to him: they felt safe with him, and it was all done in a good-humoured way. In 1993 the poet K. T. Canning wrote the following poem in his honour ('The Shelf Life of Bernard Stone' 1993).

Ode to Bernard Stone
Oh my dear Mister Stone
You've found me alone
As I browse through your store of delights.
O your eyes they beguile
And likewise your smile.
Please remove your hand from my tights.

Oh my dear Mister Stone
Do you think I'd condone
Your whispered suggestions to me?
How could you consider
I'd flash the come hither?
Kindly take your hand from my knee.

Oh my dear Mister Stone
What makes you so groan
As you fumble about in my nest?
Your glasses are steamy.
'Little flower – it's just a small test!'

Ah my dear Mister Stone
I prithee don't moan
As I move your hand from my breast
For so often your nose
Found my chest a repose
What style! What technique!
Be my guest!

When I tried to contact Ms Canning to ask her permission to publish this poem, I couldn't find her. None of my English poet friends knew of her. The English Poetry Society trawled their archives on my behalf and likewise came up with nothing. Lynn Bamber finally tracked her down: she discovered that Ms Canning is a practising artist and occasional poet now living and working in China and was delighted to hear that her poem was being republished. She gave her wholehearted permission for me to use it.

My reasons for trips to London were akin to Benedict Kiely's reasons: to see Bernard and spend time in the Turret Bookshop.

There was usually an attractive lady assistant sitting behind a table just inside the entrance. At the rear of the shop there was a small glass-fronted office — Bernard's inner sanctum, as he called it, where he held court to all and sundry, sometimes wandering into the main shop when someone expressed an interest in a particular book. Some of his friends called his office 'the archives', which was quite apt as it was full of books, manuscripts and papers, mostly referring to poetry. There was never any pressure to buy; instead Bernard was happy to talk about any book mentioned. The range of prices of the books on offer was very wide but he had a policy of welcoming small spenders, on the theory that small spenders sometimes become big spenders. He had a photograph of our family on the wall of his office and I now know that in many ways we were a surrogate family to him.

On these visits I would browse London bookshops in the mornings and spend the afternoons in his office, where all sorts of people, including publishers, writers, celebrated cartoonists, playwrights, publishers and collectors would wander in and talk. There was a fridge in the office and wine was poured freely for all comers. Occasionally he would gather a posse and head to the Chelsea Arts Club where the fun would continue. That would be the end of the working day. Once in the mid-eighties he introduced me to the poet Christopher Logue, who on hearing my Irish accent said 'I suppose you follow that fellow Heaney – greatly overrated, don't you think?' and walked out of the office before I could reply. This was ten years before Heaney won the Nobel Prize. Mr Logue did not endear himself to me.

Poetry readings were held in the shop every two weeks, to all of which I was invited but for practical reasons couldn't attend, much as I would have liked to. These gatherings were in the style of the old literary salon at which a classical pianist or cellist might provide the background music, though on one occasion the entertainment was provided by a belly dancer. As always, the wine flowed.

William Burroughs gave a rare reading in the shop on 1 June 1988 but one of the most famous readings ever held there had a stellar line-up that included Allen Ginsberg, Martin Bell, George MacBeth, Peter Redgrove and Gregory Corso, none of them getting paid. Some of the poets whose books were being launched were virtually unknown, and as often as not Bernard funded the book's publication. Occasionally there are poets who take the view that editors and publishers are there solely for their own benefit, and I am sure Bernard never got the thanks he deserved. Even though he was a children's writer, he was first and foremost a true man of poetry, with an immense knowledge and feel for the medium. This extended to Irish poets and their writing, and he had particular admiration for the young Heaney and for Derek Mahon. Apparently Samuel Beckett and W. H. Auden had placed great trust in him. Fiona Pitt-Kethley, whose favourite bookshop in London was the Turret, said of Bernard that 'he was a true rarity – a man who likes women and poetry.'

One day in his office Bernard introduced me to the English bibliographer Barry Miles, who he told me was then writing a book on Allen Ginsberg. Bernard and he were also putting together what was to be the definitive collection of Ginsberg's work, with a view to publishing it. When I innocently asked if the collection contained everything by Ginsberg, Bernard immediately replied 'Yes, we have everything but a pubic hair, and we are working on that'.

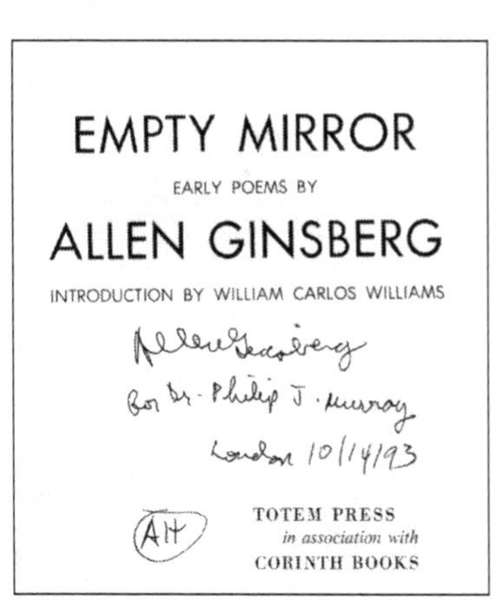
EMPTY MIRROR

EARLY POEMS BY

ALLEN GINSBERG

INTRODUCTION BY WILLIAM CARLOS WILLIAMS

Allen Ginsberg
for Dr. Philip J. Murray
London 10/14/93

AH

TOTEM PRESS
in association with
CORINTH BOOKS

In 1991 I managed to get two tickets for the second World Cup Rugby final at Twickenham and asked Bernard to join me, even though he wasn't really interested in sport. The match was between England and Australia and was the first rugby match he had ever attended. It was probably also his last. When we left the station close to the venue we saw that as usual everyone was wearing their team colours. Not to be outdone Bernard bought an English cap and scarf and I bought the Australian versions. There were Irish accents everywhere in the crowd and many such people were, like me, wearing Australian colours, hell-bent on supporting England's opponents – anything to beat the old enemy. Bernard told me afterwards that the most memorable part of the day for him was that after the game was over, with England beaten, the pubs were full of both sets of supporters happily drinking pints together and singing. He said that if it had been the soccer world cup and England had lost at home, there would have been a riot.

Bernard was no ordinary bookseller and is recognised now as being the last of a generation. He certainly fitted the description of booksellers as 'a dedicated breed, sober, cautious and impossible to excite (their assistants tend to be mousy and underpaid): a few are rude and interesting'. I am not sure where that quote comes from but surely the sober part doesn't hang well with Bernard. Dannie Abse was once asked when he first met Bernard and about remarkable meetings with him and he simply said 'All were remarkable.' Bernard's style was completely different to that of today's booksellers, who because of the immense changes that have occurred in the trade spend most of their day in front of a computer and whose main contact with customers is by e-mail and telephone. This wouldn't have suited Bernard's personality or way of life, and he may well have departed at the right time. Like everyone who is ultra generous, he knew there were those who took advantage of him but he just carried on and never bore a grudge. He would sometimes phone me to say that he had located a treasure, saying 'You must have it, dahling', and this was whether the item in question was two pounds or twenty. The price of the book was an irrelevance to him and he never overcharged. He advised me at an early stage that when I saw something special that I wanted I should buy it immediately. In the main, that is the policy I adopted, but there were occasions when the book in question was too expensive. Needless to say, when I next saw any of these books they were even more expensive and I never did get to buy them.

Bernard once phoned to say that his friend Anthony Burgess

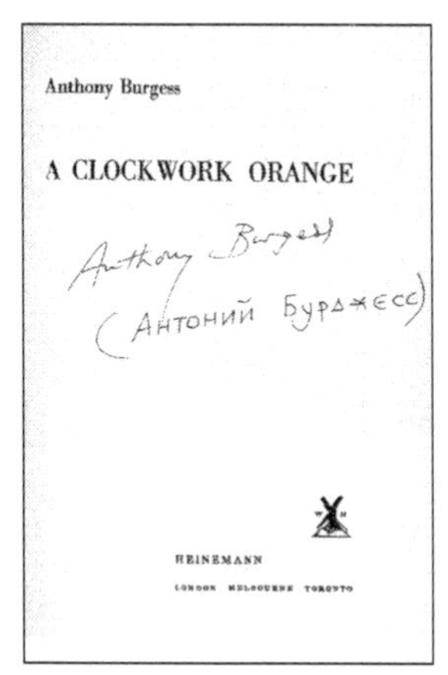
Anthony Burgess

A CLOCKWORK ORANGE

Anthony Burgess
(Антоний Бурджесс)

HEINEMANN

LONDON MELBOURNE TORONTO

would be in London the following week and if I had any of his books that I wanted signed I should send them to him immediately. I sent my copies of *A Clockwork Orange, Time for a Tiger, Enemy in the Blanket*, and *Beds in the East*, and they came back inscribed in both English and Greek. Bernard phoned again when Lawrence Durrell was due to visit and again invited me to send whatever I wanted signed. I sent *Constance, Quinx, Sebastian, Livia* and *Monsieur*, and they were duly signed.

Wherever he went, including Sligo, Bernard rummaged around in every bookshop, both new and secondhand, and found things that no one else would have found. For him, there was a home for every book and as often as not he would already have a customer waiting for his discoveries when he got back to London.

Bernard knew everyone in the literary world, and they knew him. As well as his many other attributes he was a wonderful conversationalist, with a never-ending store of literary anecdotes. I still remember spending an entire Saturday afternoon with him in one of Connolly's snugs talking about religion and politics. This Russian Jew and Southern Irish Catholic found they had no differences of opinion on the important issues, including the Arab/Israeli conflict and the one nearer home in Northern Ireland. We couldn't remember afterwards how we got on to the subject of religion, as we had never talked about it before and never did again. However, we had many other fascinating conversations on various topics over the years.

The last publishing enterprise in which Bernard was involved was a joint venture with Raymond Danowski under the Turret Press imprint that involved producing one hundred different poetry broadsides. Known as the Turret Broadsides these came out throughout 1991 and 1992. The series featured poets from all over the world and included work by Yeats, Borges, Sillitoe, Plath, Heaney, Ginsberg, Ferlinghetti, Joyce, Healy, Hoffmann, Pinter, Updike and Ted Hughes. How this particular selection of poets was arrived at I have no idea but the whole exercise was done purely for fun, as the broadsides were given away free. Some are now collector's items and a full set of a hundred would be quite valuable.

Bernard was always full of mischief, and even when he was in hospital for a lengthy period having oral surgery in the mid-seventies he never lost his sense of the ridiculous. One evening his friend Ralph Steadman had just been to see him, and on the way out met Christopher Logue on the way in. Logue continues the story: 'After entering his room, and after a word or two, there being no nurses in sight, I showed Bernard the gold top of the champagne I had in my shoulder bag. "Hunn-hun-huuuuu-uuu-hun", he said, pointing to the drawer of his bedside cupboard. Inside was a length of narrow-gauge transparent plastic tubing, supplied, as I learnt later, by Ralph Steadman. Bernard made unscrewing signs with his right hand, "discretely, discretely" with his left. It opened with a hushed pop, and before you could say "hunn-hunn", Bernard had stuck the end of the tube through his wirework, and dipped the other end into the now-concealed-by-the-bedclothes bottle.'

The Shelf Life of Bernard Stone (compiled by Camille Whitaker, printed by Lawrence Brough, 1993) was published by his friends to celebrate the bookshop's return to Covent Garden, and in 1994 a special party was arranged at the Chelsea Arts Club to celebrate his life in books. To coincide with the event, a festchrift entitled *Book 'im – 70 years on the Game* was compiled by Martina Berne and Barry Miles, with help from Ralph Steadman and Raymond Danowski. Martina said that the book was a celebration of the love and friendship Bernard had evoked in the many people he had befriended over the years. He later gave a copy to each of our three children, each one

amusingly inscribed. On Jenny's copy he wrote 'To Jenny. What! What! What! I will sue the imposter. Love Bernard.'

Vivien and I had been invited to the celebration at the Chelsea Arts Club but early that week we heard that Bernard had collapsed in his shop and been taken by ambulance to the Chelsea and Westminster Hospital. When we visited him there the next day he was sitting on a chair beside his bed with an intravenous drip in his arm and an oxygen mask over his face, looking for all the world like his beloved Inspector Mouse. He was very frail and indeed I thought he was dying. We didn't stay too long that evening and when we went again the next day I asked him if he had made enquiries about what was wrong with him. Of course he hadn't a clue what was wrong, nor would he ask – he wouldn't want to be a nuisance. As it is practically impossible to get information about a patient in hospital unless you are a blood relative I told the matron I was Bernard's general practitioner in Ireland, that I had prescribed various medicines for him over the years, and that he had given me permission to act on his behalf. She had seen the result of my handiwork on his forehead so was sufficiently convinced of my *bona fides* to take me to see Bernard's consultant. The first thing I saw in Dr Morgan's room was a large framed photograph of a famous Welsh rugby union team from the seventies, all of whose members had signed the picture. So we got on extremely well and after a passionate discussion of the state of Welsh and Irish rugby he outlined the patient's medical situation for me.

When I returned to Bernard's bedside I told him that the first four of his many serious conditions were either curable or controllable but another two were the direct result of too many Bloody Marys and too much wine, which meant that he should never drink again. He totally accepted this and never did drink again, falling back instead on cigarettes — Benson and Hedges filtered instead of his former favourites, Player's Navy Cut (until they were discontinued) and Senior Service. Some time after this illness the publisher John Calder said about Bernard: 'Always an optimist, and to all appearances in no way changed, his mind as agile as ever, he stoically accepted that the age of the individualist in the book world was over.'

Over the next few years I wrote to most of the poets who had contributed to the Turret broadside series and asked if they would sign my copy of their particular broadside. In doing this I also brought them up to date with the state of Bernard's health, thanks to information supplied by Dr Morgan. The level of genuine affection shown towards him by those who replied was quite moving. Most asked for his address so that they could write to him. A lot had lost contact and some thought he had already died. I sent him copies of all those letters afterwards and, although he never said so I got the impression he was quite pleased. Among those who wrote back to me and later signed their broadsides were Alan Sillitoe, Carol Ann Duffy, Brian Patten, Laurie Lee, Seamus Heaney, Lawrence Ferlinghetti, James Berry, Daniel Hoffman, John Ashberry and Ted Hughes. Timothy Steele wrote on his broadside 'In Passing', the following verse:

Posted from the land of Yeats
This broadside's reached the United States
With this inscription, may it hurry
Once more to Sligo and Philip Murray.

Bernard died on 3 February 2005 and his funeral service was held at Golders Green Crematorium on 15 February. Friends later told us that the mourners entered the funeral parlour to the music of Frank Sinatra's 'My Way', and that psalms were read by the cantor and poems recited by his poet friends. He got a good send-off and his niece Susan Barker penned the following poem for inclusion in the Jewish scroll for perpetuity:

A lover of the printed word
A man of few.
A believer in peace
A man who found little.
A man who saw in others
What they could not see.
A man whose immortality
Will live on in those who
Would not have achieved
Without him.

A commemoration was held in his honour at the Chelsea Arts Club on 14 April 2005 which we were able to attend. A large gathering of friends had assembled, with people coming from America and Ireland and all over England. Sigmund Freud was brought out especially for the occasion and watched over all the proceedings. We found that Bernard's English friends were aware of his many visits to Ireland over the years but knew nothing about why he had gone there. Clearly he had had many compartments to his life and had kept them separate. Poems were read by Michael Horowitz, Brian Patten, Christopher Logue and Ralph Steadman, and the publisher John Calder delivered a eulogy. It was not a sad occasion but was a typical Turret party at which all that was missing was the man himself, sitting on a throne with a Bloody Mary in one hand, a Benson and Hedges in the other, and a young lady at his side.

As an independent bookseller and publisher for nearly forty years, Bernard's record must be unique. His great legacy will be that of an extraordinary bookseller, though perhaps the last years of his life from the time of his collapse to his death should be his true legacy. After his discharge from the Chelsea and Westminster Hospital, he had recuperated in a nursing home for a few months before returning to his flat in Bloomsbury, where he lived alone. His business was essentially a one-man show and the combination of ill-health and the massive costs of running a specialist shop in central London finally combined to defeat him. Predictably he had to close the shop. He was then largely cut off from his friends; had given up alcohol; was now in involuntary retirement, and yet never once complained. He continued to have a smile on his face and see the funny side of life. We spoke on the phone on an every week basis throughout this time. He displayed extraordinary courage in great adversity and he still came to Sligo and Connolly's, where he now drank Virgin Marys instead of his normal tipple. After his death, John Hartley Williams wrote 'The disappearance of his bookshop has meant that nowhere in the whole great city of London is there a shop exclusively devoted to poetry. His shop was the last and his establishment is sorely missed.'

In the end Bernard was very much at peace with himself and the world. For me it was a great privilege to have known him and become a friend. It was always an absolute delight to be in his company. It was plainly obvious that he was a man who was true to himself and who saw the joy of life in everything he did and everyone he met. I don't mean to depict him as some kind of saint, though, because he definitely was not. He would have been greatly amused at the many glowing tributes paid in obituaries published in such newspapers as *The Times*, the *Independent*, the *Guardian*, and even the *Sydney Morning Herald*.

As well as the poems already quoted here, many others were written in his honour by, amongst others, Roger McGough, Adrian Henry, Carol Ann Duffy, Jeremy Reed, Julian Nangle, Adrian Mitchel, Edward Lucie-Smith, Michael Horowitz, Gavin Ewart, Christopher Logue, Ken Smith, Alan Sillitoe, Fiona Pitt-Kethley, and a quatrain by Seamus Heaney. However, this poem by Brian Patten seems most apt for ending this chapter as it documents the bookshop's final journey back to Covent Garden:

Bernard's Poem
All the books are whispering,
They're kicking up a fuss –
Bernard's on the move again!
Are you sure he's taking us?
We've been advertised, promoted,
We've been praised and criticised,

We've been to all the parties
But still feel unrecognised.
We're worn out, we're exhausted,
We're absolutely numbed.
From Church Walk to Lamb's Conduit Street
We've been fingered and much thumbed.
Now here we go again!
For the second time around
Our lord and master, Bernard,
Deems us Covent Garden bound.
The highly praised, the poignant,
The mediocre, the bad,
The deep ones and the shallow,
The depressing and the glad,
The books that lie in ambush,
The bitchy ones, the gruff,
The anorexic volumes,
And the ones that know their stuff –
Bernard's packing all of them,
He hasn't got the heart
To leave the duds behind him
When the time comes to depart.
His authors travel with him
In a state of mild decay,
Staggering from Lamb's Conduit Street
Bernard leads the way.
The ghosts of Harry Fainlight,
Of Durrell and the rest,
Look down at the removal vans
From their place among the blessed.
'There's a bookshop here' they whisper,
Blake's chosen the décor.
The lease goes on forever.
Your name's above the door.
Reggie's in here waiting
With an endless case of wine.
Your sister's got the cork-screw.
She says please take your time.
Bernard can hear them clearly.

He nods and bows his head.
He blows the dust from an old slipsheet,
And stores up what they've said.

From the packing-cases drift
The scents of Passion and Chanel.
Bernard's packed his second love.
The girls are moving on as well.

CHAPTER FOUR

Collecting Seamus Heaney

I have often been asked why I started to collect the writings of Seamus Heaney, or why I collected so many of them. As I mentioned earlier, I bought my first Heaney book, *North*, when I began reading poetry in 1975, and I was particularly taken with what he was writing. Why I collected so much of his writing is more complex: it must have something to do with the bibliomaniac streak I obviously possess. I never dreamt that the collection would grow to its present size. My collection contains over four and a half thousand items so you can understand the extent of the disease. The total includes Heaney's most important books in both hardback and paperback (American and English first editions), proof copies, anthologies, magazines, newspapers, translations, interviews, programmes, exhibition catalogues, recordings (audio and video), manuscripts, reviews, critical writing, portraits and ephemera of all kinds. The other author I would have liked to collect at the time was Samuel Beckett, for much the same reason. Unfortunately this was not feasible, because Beckett was world famous and most of his books were both scarce and expensive. Heaney on the other hand was an emerging writer: his books were available and, unlike now, were originally reasonably priced, particularly the early publications. For anyone to set out now to assemble such a collection of Heaney's work would be a daunting if not near-impossible task, as a lot of the early material is unavailable.

To put together an almost complete collection of any author, particularly someone as prolific as Heaney, would be impossible without the help and goodwill of other people. A key moment in my Heaney collecting was being introduced to Jim O'Halloran over twenty-five years ago. Jim is originally from Limerick and after getting an engineering degree in University College Galway he travelled the world before finally settling in

Connecticut, where he lived until his death. He was a fluent Irish speaker who during his time in Galway shared a flat with the writer Brendan O'Hehir. Jim was always a reader and had a particular interest in Irish literature, particularly poetry. Like me, he had become a collector by accident. I was introduced to him by Bernard Stone in Connolly's pub – where else? Jim had known Bernard for many years before I did and had bought a lot of books from the Turret Bookshop. Bernard was due for one of his Sligo visits and arranged for Jim to arrive at the same time so that we could all meet. I am sure Jim was as concerned as I was that things mightn't work out but we hit it off right away, realising we were both on the same wavelength.

Jim and I remained close friends until his unexpected death in November 2010. We helped each other in our respective collecting areas (not just Heaney) in every possible way. He was one of the most knowledgeable people about Irish literature I know of and he built a very fine collection of twentieth-century literary fiction and poetry, including a major Heaney collection. The real benefits for both of us emerged as time went by, as Jim was able to source the American scene and I was able to do likewise in Ireland. It was Jim who was on hand to get me American first editions and proof copies of Heaney's books as well as those of other authors I collected. Everything to do with my book collecting would have been different otherwise. With Bernard in charge of the English scene, not much happened that we weren't able to cover between us. You could say that Bernard was the orchestrator of all of this. It is now obvious that without Bernard and Jim and the three-pronged way in which we approached collecting I couldn't have put together such a near-complete collection.

Jim had a holiday home in Connemara which he visited a couple of times every year. As often as not Bernard would arrive at the same time, with the inevitable lady in tow, and after spending a few days in Sligo the three of them would go off to Jim's place. Like Bernard, Jim was a great conversationalist and obviously most of our talk centred around books. We often spent an entire afternoon in front of the fire in the back room of my house talking books. The children would say 'Mr O'Halloran and Dad are playing with their books again.' After

Bernard, Jim has been the person of most influence to me in book collecting. As they say, 'He is the wise old head', and was the first person I asked for an opinion or advice on anything concerning books.

Having read my copy of *North* in 1975 I wanted to get Heaney's three earlier books, *Death of a Naturalist, Door into the Dark,* and *Wintering Out*. They were readily available in every bookshop at the published price and I bought each of them in first English edition in both hardback and paperback. Later I also bought the American first edition of each. Heaney's first publication, however, was an early pamphlet, *Eleven Poems*. This had been published in Belfast in 1965 and was quite a flimsy item. When I was researching for this book, I came across a catalogue from the seventies that listed the copy that I bought for 14 shillings.

The next step in my collecting involved hunting down the journals, anthologies, literary magazines and newspapers in which the poems from each of the published collections had first appeared. This was where the disease started in earnest. I didn't realise at the time that I was starting out on my third complete author collection. Nor did I realise that the experience I had gained putting together my collections of Patrick White and

Liam O'Flaherty would stand me in good stead. During those years I had built up a lot of contacts with book dealers all over the world, which made life easier for the task ahead. Of course all of this took place before the advent of the internet, so it was a hard but enjoyable slog. Heaney became more widely known and more widely read than White and O'Flaherty, not just in Ireland but internationally, so more people were likely to collect his work, as turned out to be the case. On top of that, his output was much greater than that of the other two, because as well as his books he was contributing poems, reviews and articles to literary journals all over the world, leading to an enormous amount of collectible material. Even now it would be easier and less expensive to put together a complete author collection of White or O'Flaherty or most other twentieth century writers than to do this for Heaney. In every sense I was taking on a serious challenge but it proved to be an enjoyable one.

The practice of publishing poems in literary journals anything up to two years before they are collected in a book is normal. The journal contributions are the true first printings of the poems and are therefore important to collectors. The Acknowledgements section of *North* includes a list of journal sources, among them *Antaeus, The Arts in Ireland, Causeway, Encounter* and numerous others, including various anthologies. Some of these I had never heard of before but soon discovered that they were all published in Ireland, England or America and were mostly available for a few shillings each. Interestingly, in spite of everything that has happened to publishing, including recessions, many of these publications are still going strong. The American publications are mostly issued by the English departments of the principal universities. When I ordered a particular issue I was often sent a copy without charge. A form was always enclosed in the hope that I would sign up for a subscription, as I did on a few occasions. As each successive book by Heaney was published I went through the same procedure of hunting down the journal contributions and was generally successful in getting the items I wanted. Of course it is easier to track down copies of current journals than earlier editions.

By this time my storage space was coming under severe pressure, so various wardrobes and bookcases throughout the

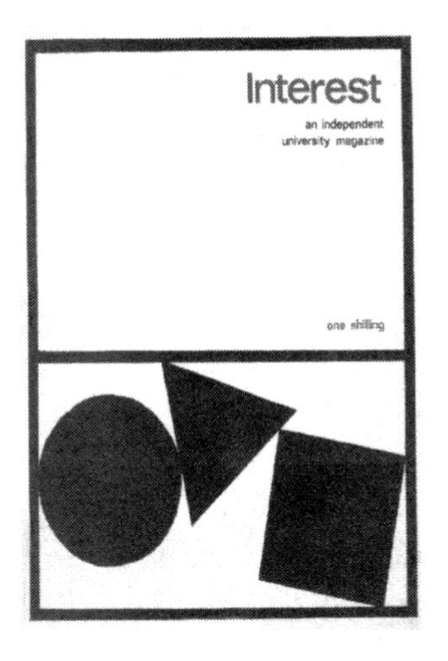
Interest
an independent
university magazine
one shilling

The
Northern
Review
a quarterly magazine
of the arts
volume one number two
five shillings
PETER REDGROVE The Old White Man NEW IRISH POETRY Seamus Heaney Michael Longley Derek Mahon Joan Newmann Stewart Parker | TOM CURRIE The Rock-Pool Girl | PAUL SMYTH Phelim O'Rourke | B S JOHNSON Holes, Syllabics &c RAYMOND WARREN A Composer's Notebook PHILIP HOBSBAUM Joyce Cary EAMONN McCANN Sam Thompson GEORGE MacCANN Louis MacNeice BOOK REVIEWS

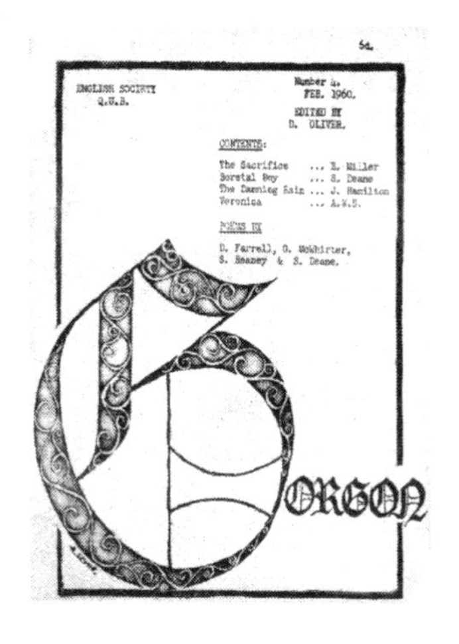
6d.
ENGLISH SOCIETY
Q.U.B.
Number 4.
FEB. 1960.
EDITED BY
D. OLIVER.
CONTENTS:
Borstal Boy ... S. Deane
Veronica
POEMS BY
D. Farrell, G. McWhirter,
S. Heaney & S. Deane.
GORGON

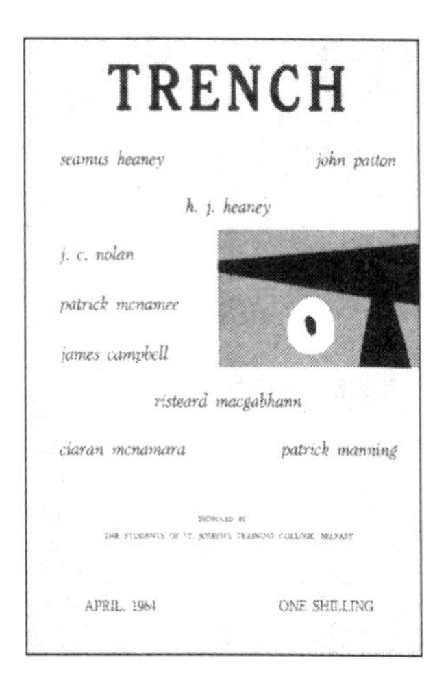
TRENCH
seamus heaney
john patton
h. j. heaney
j. c. nolan
patrick mcnamee
james campbell
risteard macgabhann
ciaran mcnamara
patrick manning
APRIL, 1964
ONE SHILLING

house were commandeered. A collector friend once told me that he had boxes of rare journals and newspapers stacked in the space under his stairs and was asked by one of his children 'What are those boxes of old newspapers doing under the stairs? Are you not going to throw them out?' That question hasn't been put to me yet.

Though neither of us knew it to begin with, it is now evident that Jim O'Halloran and I were two of the earliest serious Heaney collectors, and we have come to realise that we were fortunate to have so much material available to us. Early ephemera from Queen's University Belfast such as *Q*, *Gorgon* and *Interest*, as well as the April 1964 issue of *Trench* (published by the students of St Joseph's Training College, Belfast), where many of Heaney's earliest poems appeared, are rarely if ever seen nowadays. If they do turn up they are usually in poor condition and ridiculously priced and are bought up quickly by libraries or private collectors. These are fragile items, usually stapled together on poor-quality paper, so many of them have failed to survive the passage of time.

The Michaelmas 1959 issue of *Q* published 'Reaping in Thought' and 'October Thought', the first Heaney poems to be published. There is no record of how many copies of this issue were printed and I have never been able to find a copy. In some of the issues of *Gorgon* Heaney wrote under the pseudonym Incertus, which in an interview with the poet Dennis O'Driscoll he described as having to do with a lack of writerly self-confidence (*Stepping Stones: Interviews with Seamus Heaney*, 2008, Faber and Faber). Other early poems were written under the name Seamus J. Heaney, and the first recorded contribution under his own name is 'Lines to myself', published in the December 1960 issue of *Gorgon*. I managed to get three of the five relevant issues of *Gorgon* that contained a Heaney poem as well as one each of the *Trench* and *Interest* issues. That was a long time ago and I haven't seen a copy of any of these publications since then.

Two other early Northern Ireland literary journals were *Everyman* and *The Northern Review*. Three issues of *Everyman* that included Heaney material were published in 1968, 1969 and 1970 while two issues of *The Northern Review* in 1965 and 1967 had Heaney contributions. Like the other literary journals listed

Dermot Healy – fellow Sligo resident, 2010. *Photo: Dallan Healy*

The Kenny brothers – Conor, Tom and Des, Kenny's Bookshop, Galway. *Photo: Dean Kiely*

Bernard Stone in Sligo in the early eighties.

Photo: Vivien Murray

The witching hour in Connolly's pub. John Gault, the author, David Gunne, Bernard Stone, Lorna Gault, Gerry Nicholson, Proprietor and friend, Martine Beirne and Vivien Murray. *Photo: Unknown*

The author with John McGahern at the Hawkswell Theatre, 1985.
Photo: The Sligo Weekender

The BFG, or Big Friendly Giant that was Roald Dahl meeting the author's children, Emily, Jenny and Joe, in Kenny's Bookshop 1998.
Photo: Vivien Murray

Jim O'Halloran, kindred spirit, friend, book collector, cheese lover and, most importantly, a fellow Munster man, Connecticut 2005. *Photo: Des Lally*

The author being shown around Cuernavaca's Aztec ruins by Mexican poet Pura López Colomé, 2006. *Photo: Vivien Murray*

The author with Australian poet Les Murray – doing our bit for Australian-Irish relations, Sligo, June 2000. *Photo: Vivien Murray*

The author with fellow book collectors Kevin Whelan, Pat Brennan and Des Lally at Ballynahinch Castle, 2011. *Photo: Vivien Murray*

Seamus Heaney with the author at Phil Kelly's exhibition in the Hillsboro Art Gallery, Dublin 2005. *Photo: Alberto Darszon*

David Hammond, Belfast. Teacher, writer, musician, singer, broadcaster, publisher, documentary film-maker and friend. *Photo: Unknown*

Laurence Ferlinghetti with the author at the Coney Island signpost, Sligo, 2000. *Photo: Chris Felver*

The author, Laurence Ferlinghetti and photographer Chris Felver disembarking at Rosses Point after visiting the original Coney Island, 2004. *Photo: Karl Brennan*

The author with Cormac McCarthy in a country for old men/ in the company of old men – Cormac in a flying visit to Sligo in 2004. *Photo: Vivien Murray*

The author with Peter Fallon, poet and publisher, 2011. *Photo: Vivien Murray*

above, these are also much sought after but seldom seen. Literary journals such as *Dubliner, The Spectator, Outposts, New Statesman* and *The Listener* also contained some of Heaney's earliest poems and could be bought quite cheaply. Newspapers to which he contributed, on the other hand, were extraordinarily difficult to get unless they were bought on the day of publication. The *Belfast Telegraph* printed a lot of his early poems but I never saw a copy of a relevant issue.

Book dealers in Ireland, England and America began to take notice of Heaney in the late seventies and early eighties. Many started to specialise in selling his books and prices for his early material started to rocket. The doyen of dealers in this genre was the late Peter Jolliffe, who ran the well-known Ulysses Bookshop in Bloomsbury. He had been a first edition specialist for many years but by this time his catalogues contained an entire section called Heaneyland. Previously he had listed perhaps ten to twenty Heaney items but in Heaneyland anything up to three hundred items appeared, including everything from proof copies to ephemera. These catalogues were a treasure trove for those looking for Heaney material and Jolliffe became a worldwide authority in this area. The secondhand book market was also thriving in Dublin and Belfast, with a few outlets in Galway and Cork, and I often picked up bargains in the strangest of places. The many bookshops on Dublin's quays were fertile grounds where I bought a lot of memorabilia for a shilling or sixpence.

As mentioned above, *Eleven Poems* is one of Heaney's most elusive items. To complicate matters there were three different issues. The first issue was printed on cream laid paper and has a 9-point sun symbol in purple on the cover. The second was printed on white wove paper and has a 10-point sun symbol in blackish purple on the cover. The third has green card covers with a design of herald with drum and trumpet on the front. Obviously the first issue is the most desirable for a collector but it is also the scarcest and the most expensive. Many collectors, however, are happy to have any one of the three issues.

The *Eleven Poems* pamphlet is one of a series known as the Belfast Festival pamphlets which were published in conjunction with the Belfast Festival run by Queen's University from 1965 onwards. The other poets included in the series were Michael Longley with *Ten Poems,* Derek Mahon with *Twelve Poems,* Arthur Terry with *A Small War and Other Poems,* Joan Newman with *First Letter Home,* Philip Hobsbaum with *Snapshots,* Stewart Parker with *The Casualty's Meditation,* James Simmons with *Ballad of a Marriage,* Seamus Deane with *While Jewels Rot,* Laurence Lerner with *Spleen,* John Montague with *Home Again,* Norman Buller with *Thirteen Poems,* John Hewitt with *Tesserae,* Arthur Terry with *The Sacrifice,* Norman Dugdale with *The Disposition of the Weather,* James Simmons with *Ten Poems,* Iain Crichton Smith with *At Helensburgh,* Stewart Parker with *Maw,* and George Mackay Brown with *Twelve Poems.* The series was of huge importance as these were the first publications by Heaney, Longley, Mahon, Newman, Parker, Simmons and Deane. Like the three issues of *Eleven Poems,* some of the others also had different issues. Getting a full set of these pamphlets in their various issues presented a serious challenge.

Most of these poets were members of the Belfast Group which was started by Philip Hobsbaum. The group met at his flat, and later at Heaney's flat, to read and discuss their poetry every week. Others who attended these sessions included Paul Muldoon, Ciaran Carson, Bernard MacLaverty, Frank Ormsby and the critics Edna Longley and Michael Allen. Heaney said about the group that 'they used to talk poetry day after day with an intensity and prejudice that cannot but have left a mark on all of us.' Hobsbaum was the catalyst, just as he had been when he set up the very similar informal association of writers, mostly poets, known as The Group in London in 1953.

The Belfast Festival pamphlets have become collectors' items and, as well as the different issues, all sorts of other variations are involved, with some pamphlets printed on different kinds of paper and with different watermarks. Nobody seems to know the exact history of these publications. On top of that, only small numbers were printed, not many of which have survived to the present day. They were quite easily found throughout the seventies and eighties, though, and I managed to get a full set. Over the following years I got all the writers to sign the pamphlets that included their work. They all subsequently became household names.

Phoenix was a specialist poetry magazine published quarterly from 1967 to 1975 by Harry Chambers. Chambers was also the director and founder of the Peterloo Poets imprint, which was recognised as one of the great small presses of the late twentieth century. He gained a national and international reputation over the years. *Phoenix* was the earliest non-Irish literary journal that consistently published Heaney's work. Eight of his poems were published in the magazine during its existence. Chambers started the Phoenix Pamphlet Poets in 1968 with the intention of focusing on the work of unknown poets of quality. Glynn Hughes' *Love on the Moor* was the first in the series and the edition of one thousand copies sold out very quickly. One reviewer said at the time 'there may be no new Philip Larkin in these Phoenix Pamphlet Poets, yet Harry Chambers has grouped together a number of writers of promise' (Chambers was a devoted fan of Larkin).

Time would show that Chambers indeed did not unearth another Larkin but that his judgement about who he published was correct, particularly regarding the Irish triumvirate of Heaney, Longley and Mahon, who between them went on to win every poetry prize possible. Among the Phoenix Pamphlet Poets were Longley (*Secret Marriages*, 1968), Heaney (*A Lough Neagh Sequence*, 1969) and Mahon (*Ecclesiastes*, 1970). Between 1968 and 1972 eighteen pamphlets appeared, the other published poets being John Ashbrook, Harold Massingham, Jim Burns, John Mole, Patrick Henry, Christopher Pilling, George Kendrick, Stanley Cook, Jack Marriot, David Howarth, Eddie Wainwright, Peter Scupham, Stuart Evans and Tony Curtis. As well as the regular editions of one thousand copies, there were also signed limited editions of fifty copies of the pamphlets in hard covers, each signed by the writer. It was easy enough to get the regular edition of these pamphlets and I acquired a complete set. As I hadn't heard of a lot the writers previously, tracking them down to get them to sign their copies was difficult and it was quite a few years before I could complete that project.

One of the contributing poets, Jack Marriott, wrote to me on 8 July 1987 saying 'Dear Doctor Murray, in haste. Your note was a flattering surprise. Of course I'll be delighted to sign your copy of *A Special Illness*. I must confess to being rather curious as to how that copy has reached you in Ireland. And how you managed to track me down is another cause for wonderment. However, I must not be so inquisitive as to be impolite! Again, I'll be pleased to do as you ask. Forget the postage, as your interest is more payment than enough. Best Wishes, Jack Marriott.' I also managed to buy a copy of the limited signed edition of Heaney's *A Lough Neagh Sequence*. The ordinary edition of this pamphlet turns up in book catalogues reasonably often but the limited signed edition is rarely seen and remains one of Heaney's most elusive items.

As well as the early Queen's University journals already mentioned, Heaney also contributed to Northern Ireland journals such as *Threshold, Fortnight* and, in particular, *The Honest Ulsterman*, in whose second issue in June 1968 'Bachelor Deceased' was published, with many other poems later on. I was able to buy all of these at the time of publication. The same cannot be said for the prestigious *New Yorker*, in which Heaney has published nearly thirty poems since the first, 'Aubade', appeared in November 1971. Without the keen eye of Jim O'Halloran I would probably have missed most of these.

Apart from being one of the major poets of his generation, Heaney is also an outstanding literary critic and a playwright, lecturer and broadcaster. His experience as a teacher at Carysfort College, Blackrock, and at Oxford and Harvard, and the many poetry workshops he has conducted around the world have helped him as a reader of poetry, because he comes across as a natural and vibrant performer. He has collaborated with many musicians, most notably the uilleann piper Liam O'Flynn. Their joint performances are a sell-out wherever they go.

Heaney is one of the most translated writers in the world, having so far been published in more than thirty different languages, with German, Italian and Spanish the main ones. After publication the translations in these three languages may appear for sale in catalogues or on the internet. Translations into more obscure languages, however, present a major problem for collectors, who hear about them either by word of mouth from fellow collectors or from specialist dealers. In 2000 I heard about a Greek translation of Heaney's *Alphabets* by Stratis Haviaris and Manolis Savidis. I am not sure how or where I heard about this but once I knew about it I contacted a bookshop in Athens and was delighted to hear it had copies for sale. When I received the book I realised that it was one of a limited edition of two hundred and fifty copies but that there was also a further limited edition of twenty-four illustrated copies in a custom-made slip case, all of them signed by Heaney, Dimitris Hatzis (the engraver) and Stratis Haviaris. My Athens contact told me there was only one copy left and naturally I bought it. It would be impossible to describe it adequately, except to say that it is truly exquisite and without doubt one of the most beautiful books I have ever seen. I had a serious rush of adrenaline after I opened the parcel from Athens.

When any of my family or friends go abroad, particularly to an exotic destination, they are given the job of visiting local bookshops and checking if there are any Heaney translations for sale. John Gault, my fishing partner of thirty years, was on a visit to Reykjavik some years ago and managed to get a copy of *Penninn Hvassi* which translates into English as 'The Sharp Pen' and is in fact a compendium of poems from Heaney's first nine books.

In September 2010, I attended a medical conference in Reykjavik, and naturally found time to do the rounds of the local bookshops. Amongst other things, I enquired if there were any further Icelandic translations of Heaney's work since *Pennin Hvassi* was published in 1995. Nobody was able to help me but

our courier offered to make enquiries on my behalf. True to her word, she contacted me next day to let me know that *Pennin Hvassi* was in fact the only Icelandic translation of Heaney's work. She went on to say that Karl Gugmundsson, the translator of Heaney's work, was a friend of hers, and that she had contacted him to get the above information. When he heard the reasons for her enquiry, he suggested that we meet – and we did.

The meeting was arranged for the Dubliner pub, in the centre of Reykjavik for 5 pm the following day. He was a man of 86 years of age, and I would suspect he was in the early stages of Alzheimers disease. It was a most appropriate venue for such a meeting, because as we sipped our Guinness, we had Luke Kelly singing Irish ballads in the background.

He talked at length, and with great affection about meeting Heaney many years ago after one of his readings in Reykjavik. He was both amazed and delighted that I had a copy of his translation, and was curious to know how I had come by it. Before he left that evening we both read a few of Heaney's poems from a copy of *Sweeney Astray* that Karl had brought with him. He was a charming man, and asked to be remembered to Heaney when I returned to Ireland – which of course I did.

With this kind of help I have so far managed to get translations in twenty-eight different languages, some of which I would otherwise never have heard. It is incredible to think that some of Heaney's books have been translated in such countries as Albania, Columbia, Hungry, Israel, Japan, Korea, Lithuania and Russia.

Early in 2000 the *Sunday Independent* carried a report of a book launch that had taken place at the Mexican embassy in Dublin the previous weekend. The book was *El Nivel*, a translation of Heaney's *The Spirit Level*. The launch was chaired by the then Mexican ambassador to Ireland, Daniel Dultzen, and the reporter stated that also in attendance were Heaney himself and the translator Pura Lopez Colome. Pura is one of the foremost poets in Mexico and in 2008 was awarded the country's most prestigious poetry award, the Xavier Villaurrutia Prize. As well as having six volumes of her own poetry published by 2000, she had previously translated four of Heaney's books, including *Isla De Las Estaciones, Viendo Visiones, Tres Ensayos* and *Al Buen*

Entendor, into Mexican Spanish. As recently as April 2009 she published *El Sonnetos,* the only collection that brings together all of Heaney's sixty-one sonnets in one book. Fortunately the book is bilingual, so non-Spanish speakers like me can read it.

When I phoned the Mexican embassy in 2000 to ask where I could buy a copy of *El Nivel,* I was put through to the ambassador himself. After a long conversation about Heaney's poetry and Irish literature in general he said 'You must have a copy of the book.' There was no question of being allowed to pay and soon afterwards it arrived in the post. My love affair with Mexico was about to begin. When I contacted the embassy again a few months later to see how I could get copies of the earlier translations, I was informed that they didn't have any but would contact the translator herself in the hope that she might be able to help me. Soon afterwards Pura emailed me to say that she had spare copies of all the books and was putting them in the post for me — again without charge. She also said that she was a committed hibernophile who had been to Ireland on several occasions and felt it was time for another visit. Heaney was due to read at the Yeats Summer School in August that year and when I told her this she said she was on the way.

Vivien and I decided to offer Pura accommodation for her week's stay in Sligo. In retrospect this was probably a risky undertaking for all concerned: we knew nothing whatever about each other and the visit could have been a disaster. A few days before she was due to arrive, I contacted her to arrange how we could recognise each other at Sligo railway station. She said I should hold up a placard with the words 'Waiting for Godot' on it, so that is what I did. All went smoothly and I took her straight to Connolly's pub to introduce her to the local scene before we went home. After, I drove our visitor to the Hawkswell Theatre, where the Summer School was in progress, every day on my way to work. She attended all the lectures and, being the outgoing person she is, got to know a lot of people. Each night we went to poetry readings, including the one by Heaney, whom she was delighted to meet again.

All in all Pura's visit was an outstanding success. Apart from the literary involvement, she had a scenic tour of the area and was also greatly impressed with Connolly's, bemoaning the fact that she didn't have such a convivial hostelry near her home in Mexico. Before she left Sligo, she invited Vivien and myself to visit Mexico and two years later we did just that, staying with her family in Cuernavaca, about an hour and a half from Mexico City. We got the royal tour of the Aztec ruins and the city itself. We also met some of Pura's literary and artistic acquaintances, including the well-known Irish painter Phil Kelly, who lived in Mexico City. We attended a poetry reading that was an intriguing event for us as it was of course in Mexican Spanish. Phil unfortunately died in 2010.

Apart from the Queen's University journals and the others already mentioned, Heaney contributed a lot of his earliest poems to other literary publications of the sixties and seventies. The *Kilkenny Magazine* published sixteen issues between 1960 and 1970, four of which included his poems. The most influential of these early periodicals, however, was *Poetry Ireland*, edited by John Jordan. Eight issues were published between 1962 and 1968, and apart from Heaney there were contributions from Longley, Montague, Tom McIntyre and a young John Banville. This was the forerunner of *Poetry Ireland Review*, which recently published its one hundredth issue. John Jordan continued as editor for the first seven issues of the new series and since then the editorship has changed about a dozen times.

Building a full set of periodicals adds an extra dimension to a collection and I tried to get a complete set of all of the periodicals to which Heaney contributed. Sometimes the process took years to complete. The items were not expensive but the magazines were published in small print runs and therefore became scarce very quickly. Collecting full sets of literary periodicals can be a frustrating business, particularly trying to get the very early issues. Apart from Heaney's own contributions, the publications contain numerous reviews and critical articles about his writing by contemporary poets and critics, both Irish and international. This all adds to the importance of these publications. I am still trying to complete my collection of a few periodicals such as *University Poetry*, an English literary review of the sixties.

Trying to complete the set of *Poetry Ireland* was very difficult and at one stage I wrote to John Jordan to see if he could help me locate the three issues I was searching for. Even though I hadn't asked him to supply them he sent me copies of each by return post. Earlier the poet Máire Mhac an tSaoi had also sent me other copies I was searching for. I then set about getting these sets signed by the individual contributors and in most instances succeeded in doing this. Bernard Stone and Jim O'Halloran were of course central to a lot of this activity, but there were individual book dealers in both Ireland and England who were also extraordinarily helpful.

In the late sixties and early seventies broadsheets were in vogue and many contained early Heaney poems. The best known were edited by Richard Ryan and Hayden Murphy. Ryan was a poet in his own right, with two volumes published in the seventies. His series of broadsheets were published for the Poetry Workshop of University College Dublin. Usually about a thousand copies were issued and these were sold for a shilling each on Saturday nights in the pubs and on the streets of Dublin. They were fragile items, almost in newspaper format, and most didn't survive. I have recollections of being offered copies to buy during this time but I wasn't interested then and obviously didn't know what was ahead of me. At one stage I wrote to Ryan, who was then living in London, and told him I was trying to locate some of these early issues. He wrote back to say that there were a few boxes of them under his bed in his mother's house in Dublin and that he would do a search when he was next in Ireland. True to his word he sent me the relevant issues later in the year, for which I was very grateful. He went on to become a diplomat, and was the Irish ambassador in turn to Korea, Japan and Spain, and now to the Netherlands.

Hayden Murphy's series of broadsheets appeared between 1967 and 1978. They were initially published in Dublin and later in Edinburgh, and were extremely difficult to find. Murphy wasn't able to help me when I wrote to him as he didn't have duplicates. I managed to get *Broadsheet*, Number Four in 1967, which contained 'Last Look', *Broadsheet*, Number Twenty-one in 1974, which contained 'Act of Union', and the 1983 issue that contained 'Davin on the Broagh Road'.

The late David Hammond was another person who assisted me greatly in my book collecting over the past thirty-five years.

He was a man with an extraordinary range of interests who started out as a teacher in Belfast and later became a documentary film-maker, a musician, a broadcaster, a writer, a publisher and a singer. When he died in 2008 the broadcaster Jeremy Isaacs referred to him as 'a poet of film'. He was often called 'the lord of misrule', which was said in an affectionate way. One of his earliest films was a documentary about his friend Seamus Heaney; another early classic was *Dusty Bluebells,* which was about children's street games in West Belfast. In 1986 he moved from the BBC and formed his own company, Flying Fox Films, with which he produced such notable documentaries as *Steel Chest, Nail in the Boot, and the Barking Dog* in 1987, about life in the Belfast shipyards, and *Beyond the Troubles* in 1994 with Brian Keenan. Heaney said of him after his death 'He was a great Ulsterman and a great Irishman, a man of rare energy, one of the transformers in Irish life. He was a courageous romantic, a true democrat, free of sectarianism, and free of ideology.'

My first contact with Hammond was in the late seventies when I wrote asking him to sign two items for me. One was a slim volume called *Room to Rhyme,* which contained early poems by Heaney and Michael Longley as well as ballads by Hammond himself. This had been published in 1968 by the Arts Council of Northern Ireland. The other item was a very rare concert programme published in 1969 called *Poets Loused with Song,* which included very early contributions by Hammond, Heaney, Longley and Derek Mahon. This was specially published for 'An entertainment for the cultural edification of the citizens and for the financial edification of the Derry Itinerant Settlement Committee.' This event took place in the City Hotel, Londonderry, on Friday 12 December 1969 and admission was five shillings. Hammond signed these two items for me, and Heaney, Mahon and Longley signed them later. *Poets Loused with Song* cost me four shillings at the time and I have only once seen a copy since then. The last major production by Hammond was *Something to Write Home About: a Meditation for Television,* by Seamus Heaney. This was published in 2001 in three different versions, all of which I bought directly from Hammond.

The signing of *Room to Rhyme* and *Poets Loused with Song* was the beginning for me of a long association with Hammond. He

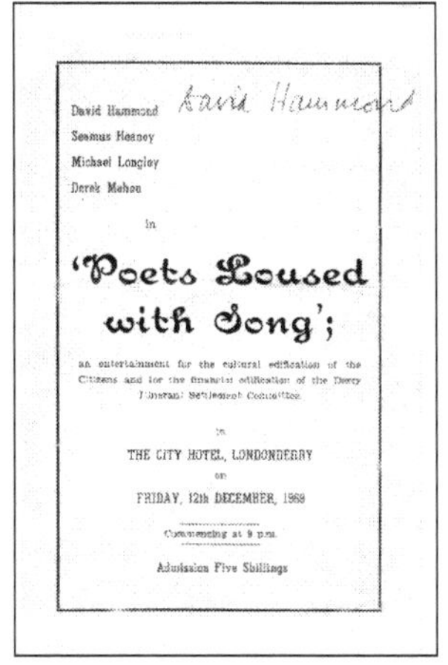

was always very helpful as well as being a wonderful raconteur. He became one of the directors of the theatrical company Field Day, founded in Derry in 1980 by Brian Friel and Stephen Rea. The other directors were Seamus Heaney, Seamus Deane and Tom Paulin, who were later joined on the board by the playwright Thomas Kilroy. Between 1982 and 1983 the company produced twelve plays, including *The Cure at Troy* by Heaney in 1990. In true theatrical fashion, each play had a gala opening in the Guildhall in Derry and then toured the country, North and South, often playing in 'unfashionable' destinations, invariably to glowing reviews. Since 1990 Heaney's *The Cure at Troy* has been produced in theatres all over the world.

The Field Day company was very much in the style of the fit-up companies of old, and the casts included some of the leading actors and actresses of the time. The programmes and posters for these productions were lavish affairs and have become much sought after. The artwork for programme frontispieces and for posters was provided by the Belfast artist Basil Blackshaw and Heaney contributed new poems to some of the programmes. All the playwrights involved in these productions were Irish apart from the South African Athol Fugard, whose *Boesman and Lena* was staged in 1983, and David Rudkin, who is of Anglo-Irish origin and whose play *Cries for Casement as his Bones are Brought to Dublin* was staged in 1992. Later I managed to get all the playwrights to sign both their poster and their programme. It was my good fortune to see all twelve plays, as the Hawkswell

Theatre in Sligo was one of the touring venues. In 1983 Field Day published Heaney's *Sweeney Astray* in both hardback and paperback and I bought both versions. These were the true first editions as the American and English first editions didn't appear until a year later.

A Field Day pamphlet series was inaugurated by the company in 1983. Fifteen pamphlets were published, three at a time, between 1983 and 1988. Each of the five sets (none were produced in 1987) had a wrap-around band and cost between £4.50 and £6.50. I bought each set as it was published. Tom Paulin, Seamus Heaney and Seamus Deane were in the first set, Robert Kearney, Seamus Deane and Declan Kiberd in the second, Terence Brown, Marianne Elliott and Robert L. McCartney in the third, Eanna Molloy, Michael Farrell and Patrick J. McGrory in the fourth, and Terry Eagleton, Frederic Jameson and Edward W. Said in the fifth and final set. These were all eminent writers or thinkers in the political sphere and each author in turn signed their pamphlet for me. The most difficult to track down was the Palestinian-American Edward Said, who was at that time Professor of English at Columbia University.

The final Field Day publication came in 1991 when the *Field Day Anthology of Writing* appeared in a three-volume set, with Seamus Deane as the general editor. This was a mammoth undertaking that engendered some controversy at the time because only a few female contributors were included. This led to volumes four and five being published in 2002 by Cork University Press. Heaney had a big part to play in the anthology, as he edited the section on W. B. Yeats in volume two and contributed sixteen poems to volume three. One of Field Day's great strengths was that, at a time when civil strife in Northern Ireland was at its peak, the governing board was composed of both Catholics and Protestants. They managed to integrate the two traditions successfully, whether in their theatrical productions or their literary publications. One English academic describes Field Day as having a board of directors made up of 'A playwright, three poets, an actor, and a walking saint', the last being Hammond. Between programmes, posters, pamphlets and the anthology, Field Day was to become a wonderful and important source of Heaney material for me and many other collectors.

Broadsides were popular in the sixties and seventies and sets of pamphlets were equally in vogue in the seventies and eighties, with Heaney a regular contributor. As well as the pamphlets already mentioned, *The Fire i' the Flint: Reflections on the Poetry of Gerard Manley Hopkins* was published in 1974 as one of the British Academy's Chatterton Lectures on Poetry. This series consisted of thirty-one pamphlets, published yearly from 1955 to 1985. I managed to get a full set of all except three of the earliest publications. *The Making of a Music* by Heaney was published in 1980 as one of the Kenneth Allott Lectures. There were eight pamphlets in this series and again I was able to get a full set. The best known among other pamphlet series of the time was the John Malone Memorial Lectures whose first publication was Heaney's *Among Schoolchildren* in 1983. This set included six pamphlets, the last being David Hammond's *Recollection* and I acquired all of them at the time of publication. Unlike the early pamphlets these frequently turn up on the internet and in catalogues.

As we all know, Heaney went on to win the Nobel Prize in October 1995, and most would agree that his win was not before its time. Hammond was one of a small number of Heaney's guests at the ceremony in Stockholm in December when he delivered his Nobel Lecture, *Crediting Poetry*. Everyone present was given a copy of the lecture, which was published in both English and Swedish and presented in loose sheets. Hammond, true to form, managed to acquire a few extra sets, which he later told me were left behind on people's chairs after the ceremony was over. When he returned to Ireland he had one of these sets specially bound by the well-known Belfast binder Sydney Aiken and inscribed it to me before getting Heaney do likewise and then he presented it to me. For sentimental rather than economic reasons, it is one of my most prized possessions. Gallery Press later published the lecture in book form and it was then published in both America and England, but the one from Stockholm is the true first edition.

When Heaney was announced as the winner of the prize in October I happened to be in Brussels attending a medical conference. I immediately phoned Vivien in Sligo, breaking our long-standing arrangement not to phone each other when either of us is out of the country, except in the event of an emergency. When she took my call that evening she immediately said 'I presume you want me to buy all the newspapers', which of course was exactly why I was contacting her. Brussels was a useful place to be that weekend as I was able to buy newspapers and magazines from all over the world. Each of these carried a leading article on Heaney as well as some of his poems and numerous critical writings. These publications were also in many different languages and I had to buy an extra suitcase to bring them home.

As well as contributing to literary journals, magazines and anthologies, Heaney has written literary criticism and poetry for newspapers worldwide. Unfortunately, apart from those published in America, where Jim O'Halloran kept a watching brief, many of these are too difficult for me to obtain. Current Irish and English newspapers, though, are easy to keep track of and are inexpensive if they are bought at the time of issue. There are specialist dealers in England and America who carry large stocks of old newspapers, with special emphasis on major world events, but they tend to be expensive and only erratically available. Occasionally a dealer will catalogue a major run of a particular newspaper. This usually happens when someone is moving house and wants to dispose of what they regard as a load of rubbish, so bargains can be got. My mother-in-law in Sydney plays her part, too, sending me relevant copies of Australia's principal newspapers, the *Sydney Morning Herald* and *The Australian*. When I get a newspaper with a Heaney contribution I keep the whole issue, which of course adds to my ongoing storage problem.

Few writers anywhere in the world have collaborated with fellow writers and artists as much as Heaney has. The two anthologies that he edited with Ted Hughes, *The Rattle Bag* in 1982 and *The School Bag* in 1997, are major examples. These two books are now on the school curriculum. The sheer number of people Heaney has been involved with is too large to document but it is worth listing some of the more artistic collaborations. These include *Keeping Going* with illustrations by Dimitri Hadzi, *Ugolino* with two lithographs by Louis Le Brocquy, *Bog Poems* with illustrations by Barrie Cooke, *Colmcille the Scribe* with calligraphy by Tim O Neill, Dante's *Inferno* with a frontispiece by Francesco Clemente, *Squarings* with forty-eight drawings by Sol Lewitt, *Squarings* with four lithographs by Felim Egan, *Hedge School* with four woodcuts by Claire Van Vliet, *Eight Irish Writers* with eight charcoal drawings by Louis Le Brocquy, *The Light of the Leaves* with a screen print by Jan Hendrix, *Sandymount Strand* with etchings by Felim Egan, *Glanmore Sonnets* with Cecil King, *Poems and a Memoir* illustrated by Henry Pearson, and *The Testament of Cresseid* with images by Hughie O'Donoghue.

These books were published in limited editions with beautiful bindings, and most are in slipcases. They are signed by both Heaney and the artist involved, and many are published abroad. They rarely come into the public domain, so very few people see them. Such editions are usually oversubscribed before publication and generally end up in libraries and private collections. Like many rare books that end up in such circumstances, in many ways they can be said to be lost to the world. If great private collections weren't sometimes broken up and sold, these books would never become available to the public or to modern collectors. There are many more publications like the ones mentioned here and this short list gives some idea of the difficulties collectors have. If you have no prior knowledge of such publications they become unobtainable because they disappear from the market so quickly

Exhibition catalogues and programmes of all kinds are another area of collaboration for Heaney and it is another area that is difficult to keep up with. Heaney's poem 'Markings' even appeared in the programme for the 1993 All-Ireland football final, which was the last time his native County Derry played in the final. When you add in all the introductions, forewords, afterwords, blurbs, etc that he has contributed to more than one hundred and fifty books and anthologies from round the world, the enormous task of collecting Heaney becomes clear. There are also audiocassettes of his books such as *Station Island, The Spirit Level, Stepping Stones, Beowulf,* and the recent documentary, *Out of the Marvellous*. These cassettes are easy to buy, but I have only managed to get a random selection of other broadcasts.

Heaney has taken part in joint readings with fellow poets

such as Derek Mahon, John Montague, Nuala Ní Dhomhnaill, Joseph Brodsky, Derek Walcott, Michael Longley and many others. Some of these events have led to joint publications that have become collectors' items, the best known of which are *An Upstairs Outlook* with Michael Longley in 1989, *In Their Element* with Derek Mahon in 1977, and *50/60: A Reading to Mark the Sixtieth Birthday of John Montague and the Fiftieth Birthday of Seamus Heaney* in 1989. I had the pleasure of attending this reading in Dublin's Gate Theatre. Heaney's most recent collaboration was with fellow Northern Ireland poet Michael Longley in conjunction with the Ulster Orchestra at Belfast's Waterfront Theatre on 17 October 2009. This was a joint celebration of the seventieth birthdays of the two poets and the hall was full to its capacity of over two thousand. Apart from the commercial records and videos mentioned above, Heaney is in constant demand for radio and television, particularly for such programmes as RTÉ's *The Arts Show, Bowman's Saturday, Artzone* and *Rattlebag* and the BBC's *Front Row* and *Booked*. It is difficult to keep abreast of such productions but I have managed to accumulate about sixty recordings in total.

I have mentioned that Heaney is regarded as one of the best readers in the world and as a result is in constant demand. No matter how large the auditorium his readings are invariably sell-outs – he has almost reached pop star status and is regarded as the most widely read living poet in the English language. In 2010, as well as his international commitments, he read almost every week at various literary festivals all over Ireland. In America most of his readings take place in universities, usually coinciding with the conferring of an honorary doctorate. Sometimes a pamphlet or broadside is published to mark the occasion. These are issued in limited numbers and tend not to be known about on this side of the Atlantic until long after the event. Without Jim O'Halloran's help I would have had little chance of getting these items.

For obvious reasons, difficulties for collectors arise when such events take place outside Ireland, England or America. In 1994 Heaney was the guest of honour at the University of Tasmania in Hobart where he delivered the James McAuley Memorial Lecture. This was published in pamphlet form as

Speranza in Reading: On the Ballad of Reading Gaol. I am still not sure how I heard about it but I contacted David O'Neill, an old rugby mate and a book man, who managed to get copies for both of us from the English Department of the university. In the year 2000 *From the Back of the North Wind* was published by the Book Art Museum, Lodz, Poland, in co-operation with the British Council, in an edition of 1250 copies. When I phoned the British Council I discovered that I was talking to Cathal McCabe, a Donegal man who was director of the Council at the time, and he very kindly sent me a copy.

A similar situation arose in 2002 when Heaney was granted an honorary doctorate at Rhodes University in the Eastern Cape Province of South Africa. The occasion was to honour Malvern Van Wyk Smith, a former head of the English department at the university. Heaney's talk was entitled *Hope and History and the Guttural Muse* and again it was published in pamphlet form. My contacts didn't extend to South Africa so I wrote to the then head of the English Department at Rhodes University to ask if I could buy a copy. A few weeks later I received a letter from the Professor of English with a complimentary copy of the pamphlet as well as an audiocassette of the reading.

In 2003 Heaney and the artist Felim Egan took part in the three-hundredth anniversary of the foundation of the city of St Petersburg. A card was published for the occasion which included the poem 'Vitruviana' by Heaney and a watercolour by Egan. The card was published by Hieroglyph Editions in an edition of one thousand copies and was not on sale in conventional bookshops. I was able to buy a copy only by writing directly to the publisher. It is only now that I realise the lengths I sometimes went to in tracking down such obscure items.

I acquired some unusual items over the years. In 1996 I bought a set of ten Irish linen poetry scrolls, measuring 36 by 19 inches each. The poems in the series are 'Thatcher', 'The Errand', 'Bogland', 'Fosterling', 'The Cure at Troy', 'The First Flight', 'Tractors', 'In Memoriam Francis Ledwidge', 'From Station Island' and 'The Tollund Man'. The poems were printed on linen scrolls and featured in the Singing Schools exhibition held from 23 April to 27 June 1996 in the Lanyon room, Queen's University Centre, which is where I saw them. This is one of a limited edition of nine sets.

On 1 October 2004 a special joint stamp was issued by An Post in Dublin and Swedish Post in Stockholm. The issue was dedicated to Ireland's four Nobel Prize winners in literature, W. B. Yeats, G. B. Shaw, Samuel Beckett and Seamus Heaney. The stamps were designed by Gustav Malmfors and engraved by Lars Sjõõblom and went on release to the general public in Ireland and Sweden on the same day.

In 2005 *The Door Stands Open* by Heaney was launched by the Irish Writers' Centre in Dublin. It was limited to 250 signed copies plus a deluxe edition limited to 50 copies that were numbered with roman numerals. The production was unique as it came in a glass slipcase with a mixed-metal spine incorporating Heaney's signature. It was produced in Poland before being shipped to Ireland and was different to anything any of us had ever seen. One collector friend asked if it could really be classed as a book, or was it an artefact?

Every writer gets negative reviews on occasion and it would be remarkable if the same hadn't happened to Heaney. Critics are entitled to their opinions about books and other publications but some begrudging criticisms have been written about the man himself that had little if anything to do with his writing. In 1989 the *Daily Mail* in England published an article headed 'Seamus should be ashamed of himself'. This appeared shortly after he had been elected to the Oxford Poetry Professorship and the article was riddled with jealousy, presumably because an Irishman had won the post ahead of his English colleagues. Two years later the Dublin writer Desmond Fennell published a pamphlet entitled *Whatever You Say, Say Nothing. Why Seamus Heaney is No 1.* This led to a public outcry, with letters appearing in *The Irish Times* almost every day in April and throughout May and June, all headed 'The Heaney Phenomenon'. All the letters were in Heaney's favour. In the *Sunday Independent* on 8 October 1995, just days after the announcement that Heaney had won the Nobel Prize, critic and broadcaster Eamon Dunphy wrote a scurrilous article entitled 'Stand in line, or be called a Philistine'. Dunphy had written a similar diatribe some weeks earlier about the then President of Ireland, Mrs Mary Robinson. It was almost as if he felt honour-bound to single-handedly knock down anyone who was on a pedestal in Ireland. The only other such reference that I can recall was an article by Brigid McLaughlin in the September 1996 issue of *Punch*, entitled 'Shame on you, Seamus', which masqueraded as a review of his book *Spirit Level*. Being the wise man that he is, Heaney kept his counsel and said nothing on any of these occasions. I mention them here for posterity.

Another of those without whose advice and assistance I couldn't have compiled this collection is the poet Peter Fallon. He has published eight books of poetry and forty years ago founded The Gallery Press, one of the foremost poetry presses in these islands and one with a world reputation. The Gallery Press has published six books by Heaney, including *After Summer* (with Deerfield Press in Worcester, MA, USA) in 1978, *Hailstones* in 1984, *The Midnight Verdict* in 1993, *Crediting Poetry* in 1995, *The Riverbank Field* in 2007 and *Spelling it Out* in 2009. Most of these were signed limited editions and sold out very quickly. I managed to get a copy of each from Peter at the time of publication. Apart from giving me advice, he has kept me up to date with forthcoming publications, not just by Heaney but by other poets whose books I am interested in reading and collecting.

There are other Heaney collectors with whom I keep in touch, notably Des Lally in Galway, Pat Brennan in Dublin, and Kevin Whelan in Dublin. They are all in book collecting for the right reasons. In many ways we are like members of an elite club: we constantly share our knowledge, passing on relevant information and sometimes books. There has never been a hint of jealousy. Both Jim O'Halloran and Pat Brennan were the central figures in researching the recent publication, *Seamus Heaney: A Bibliography 1959-2003*, which was jointly written by the late Michael Durkan and Rand Brandes and launched at the Irish Writers' Centre on 5 July 2008. Jim worked on the book in a consultancy capacity, and as well as the years spent researching and correcting the text, he was responsible for the Irish language input. Pat was the curator at the Heaney centre in Bellaghy, Co Derry, and Kevin is the director of the Keough Naughton Notre Dame centre in Dublin. Like Jim and I, Des, Pat, and Kevin were readers at first and drifted into collecting.

There is a huge difference between the number of items in

my Heaney collection and the number listed in the official bibliography by Durkan and Brandes. Items that I have on critical writing, letters, non-commercial recordings, portraits and manuscripts are not included in the official bibliography. My collection also includes an enormous amount of association material and complete sets of literary periodicals such as *Poetry Ireland Review, Phoenix, The Kilkenny Magazine* and many other similar publications that are not in the official version, and finally my collection is ongoing, whereas the Durcan/Brandes version ends in 2003. Putting my Heaney collection together has been the main focus of my book-collecting life and has given me great pleasure. I also have a sense of achievement and, in spite of having had some near heart attacks along the way, I have found the venture thoroughly enjoyable and worth every second of the time it has taken.

Mr Heaney has very kindly given me the following previously unpublished poem to include here:

Tankas for Liam O Flynn

1
Security men
Puzzled by the long flat case
The piper carried,
Stopped him. 'Is that a gun,sir?'
'O worse,' he declared, 'far worse'.'

2
You don't blow into
Uileann pipes, your elbow works
A set of bellows.
Slow airs that might have breathed on
The face of the Deep Are Breathed

3
On a set of reeds
That learners learn on – how to
Run rings round themselves
First on the chanter, later
On drones and regulator.

4
Hence, writes Giraldus
Cambrensis, those very things
The most perceptive
Value the most will appear
To others disordered noise.

5
Spenser too, I thought –
Given his blast against bards –
Might have given vent
To views on pipes and pipers.
But nor a word can I find.

6
Liam O Flynn says
That the only English rhyme
For the word 'uileann' –
From Irish uile, meaning
Elbow – is the word 'villain'.

7
In Irish, the verb
Seid, meaning 'to blow', meaning
The onset of winds,
Mighty Pentecostal winds,
Also means 'to play the pipes'.

8
The solicitor
Questioned the dying master
One last time: 'You want
To leave your pipes to that man?
Why?' 'Because he can play them.'

CHAPTER FIVE

Book Launches, Readings and Signings

Many people who read or collect books like to get their copies signed at book launches or readings, or by writing to the author. The first method is the easier, as authors usually sign books at a launch or reading. This is a civilised way of doing business: as well as getting your books signed you can meet and talk to the author, and some authors are happy to discuss aspects of the book they are signing. Some people are too shy to do this, particularly if the author is someone famous, but this is a two-way thing. Authors need the reading public to buy their books as well as read them and it must be very gratifying for an author to arrive at a venue to hear that the full house sign is up. On the other hand, it can be devastating if only a dozen or so people are in attendance. However, the saying 'the show must go on' applies to book launches and readings just as it does in the theatre.

One event in Galway in the early eighties was a unique book signing by Roald Dahl at Kennys Bookshop. Dahl was then probably the best known and most widely read and loved children's writer anywhere in the world, though he also wrote adult fiction. At the time of the signing in Galway he was an elderly man and rarely attended such gatherings, but he said afterwards that he couldn't resist a children's festival. This particular signing took place in conjunction with the Galway children's street festival, and on that day the High Street and surrounding side streets were closed to traffic. Local sculptors John Behan and John Coll also demonstrated their craft throughout the afternoon in the nearby streets. The signing continued for the entire Saturday afternoon, as families had travelled from far and wide. Parents and their children, including my own family, stood in a queue which went out of the shop and right up the street. Mr Dahl had previously signed my copies of *My Uncle*

Oswald, Switch Bitch and *Kiss Kiss* and in the meantime our children had been devouring his children's books so it was a great thrill for them to meet their hero and have their photograph taken with him as well as getting their books signed. He was most impressed with our offspring as between them they had all his children's books. It was quite apparent that he got great enjoyment out of meeting the hundreds of children who queued up that day to have their books signed.

The most famous occasion at the Kenny shop, however, occurred in 1990 when the family celebrated the fiftieth anniversary of the business. The guest of honour and keynote speaker was the then President of Ireland, Dr Patrick Hillery. On the same night the Kennys launched *Faces in a Bookshop* to mark the occasion. This anniversary volume is a compendium of about one hundred and ten photographs of writers taken over the preceding fifty years when writers visited the shop. The book has since become a collector's item.

All the photographed writers who were still alive were invited to the celebration in 1990, though some couldn't make it, including John McGahern, who later said to me 'And I heard the whiskey flowed out the front door.' As soon as the formalities were over on the night of the anniversary, the various authors went round getting each other to sign their copies of *Faces* – I even had a few requests myself, though of course I wasn't in the book. People who hope to collect signatures they missed in 1990 still turn up at all sorts of gatherings at Kennys. As well as the dignitaries a large number of readers and collectors also attended the 1990 event. It was later reported that a nearby hostelry had a late night singsong led by the novelist Michael Mullen.

Reading tours are often arranged to advertise and sell a newly published book. People tend to assume that all writers will be good readers but plainly that is not the case, nor indeed should it be. John McGahern, Seamus Heaney, Carol Anne Duffy, Paul Muldoon, Paul Durcan and others nearly always read to a full house and have a great ability to empathise with their audience. To be able to read at this level is obviously a gift, and as well as giving the writer increased exposure it helps to sell more books. Some well-known writers, though, have never given a reading, for all sorts of reasons, and of course that is their right. Others are constantly on the reading circuit, which can be financially useful as expenses and a stipend are paid. But there are those for whom a reading is a nightmare or a chore that has to be endured. Such authors may even need liquid refreshment beforehand. Readings are much more sedate affairs now than when I first started going to them in the seventies, when many authors were half tight. Some of them wouldn't perform at all if they weren't well lubricated, which of course led to some hilarious situations.

Most literary readings seem to be given by poets, though I am not sure why. Of course poets have an advantage over novelists in that they can give a more balanced and varied programme, including old favourites as well as new and unpublished poems. Each poem is a separate entity that can stand on its own merits whereas a novelist has to pick out chunks to read that may have no apparent link between them.

The best prose reading I have attended was by Patrick McCabe when he read from his breakthrough novel *The Butcher Boy* at the Model Arts Centre in Sligo in 1992, shortly after the book was published. McCabe brought the book to life as he practically acted each part, particularly that of the main character Francie Brady. Before this I had had little knowledge of him or his writing and the only book of his that I had read was his third, *Carn*. I bought *The Butcher Boy* after reading a hugely complimentary review in *The Irish Times*. As well as selling extremely well this went on to become a successful stage play and film. McCabe's writing career was well and truly launched.

John McGahern was another wonderful reader, who was in every sense a born storyteller. He didn't read often but when he did it was an important event. He was another of the many Irish writers who had fallen foul of the notorious censorship law: his second novel, *The Dark*, was banned for alleged pornographic content shortly after its publication in 1965. His readings were humorous though his delivery was deadpan and he had a wry smile on his face all the time. A mutual friend once remarked that you had to be careful of what you said in his presence or you could easily appear in his next book. I suspect this applies to most writers. Over the years I have collected and read all McGahern's books and he was always very generous to me in signing them shortly after publication. He is now rightly regarded as one of the greatest writers of our time, as both a novelist and a short story writer. Interestingly, during his lifetime he was probably more widely read in France than he was in Ireland.

Dermot Healy is another entertaining reader, when his ability and experience as an actor comes to the fore. He is a poet as well as a novelist so has a choice of medium. He was probably the first Irish author whose signature I requested. At the time he was living in Brixton and wrote in a most humorous manner to say he would be delighted to oblige me and sign my copies of his earliest books, *Banished Misfortunes* and *Fighting with Shadows*. Since then he has written what I regard are his best books, *A Bend for Home* and *A Goat's Song*. He now lives in Sligo so it is easy for me to get his work signed.

Benedict Kiely was in many ways not unlike McGahern. He had a large output of both short stories and novels and was also a broadcaster of note. He too was always very good to me and signed my copies of *Nothing Happens in Carmincross, The Captain with the Whiskers* and *Proxopera,* amongst others. In 1999, in honour of his eightieth birthday, a plaque was unveiled in his honour in his native Omagh. In an interview afterwards he was asked about censorship and said 'If you weren't banned, it meant that you were no bloody good.'

Seamus Heaney's readings are legendary and he fills the largest auditoriums wherever he goes. In 2004 he was the guest poet at the Yeats Winter School in Sligo. Unlike the Yeats Summer School this is a weekend affair only, catering for about ninety people, mostly from the local area. During this particular weekend Heaney gave a prose reading entitled 'The Rite Word in the Rote Order' in the Hawkswell Theatre at midday on the Saturday. This was a serious and at the same time a humorous lecture. He provided an absolute master-class in the use of the English language and as usual he had the audience in the palm of his hand.

Later that day Heaney gave a poetry reading at the Sligo Park Hotel, again to a full house. Just as he was about to start the reading, the door of the hall opened and a member of staff helped an elderly white-haired lady down the four steps into the auditorium. All the seats were occupied so, gentleman that I am, I helped her into my seat at the front of the hall and went to sit on the floor at the back. Towards the end of the session Heaney announced that he would read two more short poems and then call it a day. At that, the mystery lady got up to leave and was assisted up the steps. The reading had stopped and all eyes in the room, including Heaney's, were on her. On arriving at the top step she turned towards the podium, bowed once and said 'Good night, Sweet Prince.' The place erupted and it took quite a while before the reading could continue. Try as we might to track her down, the lady had vanished just as mysteriously as she had arrived. We never found out who she was or where she came from.

The reading public tends to think that writers gravitate to each other's company all the time. Some indeed do, but the opposite is also the case, and occasionally there is open jealousy between them. Literary prizes can sometimes bring out the worst in writers, particularly when one of them feels that his or her book should have won the award given to someone else. William Golding and Anthony Burgess had a falling out in 1980 when Golding won the Booker Prize with *Rites of Passage*, which was up against Burgess's *Earthly Powers*. A more recent public spat erupted between Martin Amis and Julian Barnes over a change of agent. And V. S. Naipaul and Paul Theroux famously fell out when, among other things, the latter discovered that Naipaul had sold specially inscribed first editions of Theroux's books. Peter Carey was once quoted in the *Sunday Times* as saying, 'Writers are always envious, mean-minded, filled with rage and envy at others' good fortune. There is nothing like the failure of a close friend to cheer us up.' He was later quoted as saying, 'When I was writing *Illywhacker*, my friend Salman Rushdie published a bit of *Midnight's Children*. One side of me was thinking this was fabulous, the other side thinking, you bastard.' Of course this could happen in any walk of life, though perhaps particularly in modern music and sport.

Great opportunities for getting writers' signatures are provided by the literary festivals that take place all over Ireland from spring through to autumn. The major festivals are Cúirt in Galway, the Yeats International Summer School in Sligo, the Listowel Writers' Festival, the Scríobh Literary Festival in Sligo (now sadly defunct), the Clifden Arts Festival, the Poetry Now Festival in Dún Laoghaire, the Dublin Writers' Festival and as many as a dozen others. One could spend the entire season going from one festival to another but I try to attend only those where particular writers in whom I am interested are reading. In general the festival programmes are very impressive, with both national and international writers attending.

There is an ongoing debate as to whether copies signed with just the author's name or those inscribed to the owner of a book are more desirable or valuable. Generally speaking, unless the inscription has an important association of some kind, or the copy is extremely rare, serious collectors will not buy a book if it is already inscribed to someone else. An association copy is in effect a presentation copy that was the gift of the author. The main interest of any presentation copy will always be that of its association – the interest or importance of the recipient, his connection with the author or another such special recommendation. When faced with a lengthy queue of people, famous writers will sometimes decide to sign only, which takes much less time than inscribing a personal message. Seamus Heaney is one such writer but he is so generous with his time that he is often still signing long after the reading is over. Unsigned copies of his books are even said to be more valuable than signed or inscribed ones, since the first kind are comparatively rare. Getting an inscribed copy makes the whole collecting exercise far more personal: I can still remember particular occasions when I had certain books inscribed, as well as being able to remember where and when I bought those books and what I paid for them. Whenever there is a choice I like to get my books inscribed.

Unfortunately, as authors are aware, there are unscrupulous people who sell copies on to dealers soon after a signing. Once someone I knew well was in a queue for signatures ahead of me and asked the famous author to sign ten copies of the same book, which he did. A few major bookshops such as Hatchard's in London specialise in signed copies of recently published books in all disciplines. They sell them at the published price plus postage so it is an easy way of getting signed copies, and the author, the bookshop and the collector all benefit.

Contacting authors can be quite complicated as well as time-consuming and expensive. Also, some writers are difficult to track down. The Arts Council of Ireland, Poetry Ireland, Children's Books Ireland, the Poetry Society of England, the Writers' Centre in Dublin and other such bodies have personal details of many writers and artists but are not allowed to disclose their addresses or phone numbers without permission. When all else fails, the last resort is to write to the author care of the publisher, enclosing a letter to be forwarded. The matter might end there as publishers may decide not to send the letter on, especially if it hasn't got the appropriate postage stamps on it. Writing to the publisher instead can also be unsatisfactory, because if you don't hear from the author you don't know whether your letter has been passed on. Luck can also be a factor: an author in the middle of writing a book might not want to be distracted, whereas if a newly published book is being reviewed and advertised he or she will probably be quite happy to sign. In general, though, I have found that most authors are glad to sign when a request reaches them.

Of course, asking authors to provide signatures is an intrusion and they have a perfect right to refuse the request if they want. I quickly learnt that it is most important to use common courtesy when writing to ask for a signature. I adopted the policy of writing to ask permission to post a book or books before I did so. I gave the reasons for my request as well as commenting on the author's writing and offering to pay return postage. Later I learnt from some of the authors that many signature collectors just send their books without first asking for permission and even without enclosing the necessary return postage. When I received a positive reply to my requests, I calculated the cost of return postage and enclosed that amount with the books. I had obviously miscalculated when an English author on returning my books informed me that I had short-changed him. He wrote across the front of the parcel for all to see, 'You owe me thirty pence.' Naturally I made up the difference and apologised, and he signed other books for me later. Expecting a writer to pay return postage is indeed very inconsiderate but some don't seem to mind the expense: after I asked Georges Simenon to sign my copy of *Maigret Takes the Waters* he said 'Thank you for your kind letter, and to say I will autograph with pleasure your copy of the book. If you send the volume to the address noted, I shall inscribe it for you and then send it back post-haste. Please do not worry about covering postage expenses for return of the book.'

I realised something else when I asked an English poet to sign some books. He replied, 'Yes, I'll sign them and return them if you enclose a stamped addressed package for them. I have no time to be finding stuff to make parcels with, or standing in post office queues.' In January 1980 Sean O'Faolain said 'If you post the book or books, enclose twine, brown paper, and a postal order or cheque for the stamps, or best of all, the stamps for return I will be happy to oblige.' In the late seventies when I asked John Le Carré to sign my copy of *The Naïve and Sentimental Lover* he replied 'Thank you for your kind letter. I have no secretary, and like the rest of us, am only mortal, so I don't very much like wrapping parcels and taking them to the GPO. May I suggest that you accept the enclosed piece of paper with my signature on, and gum it on to the fly-leaf? Your book will suffer a lot less from handling, also! Thanks again.' In 1986 I wrote again to ask him to sign my copy of *A Perfect Spy* and on this occasion he agreed to do so, and inscribed it 'For Doctor Philip Murray, with my best wishes – and I hope it's worth the trees! John Le Carré, 30th May 1986.' He again obliged me in 1989 when he signed my copy of *The Russia House*. An interesting aside here is that the headed notepaper for his 1986 letter had 'John Le Carré' at the top of the page, whereas his 1989 letter had his real name, David Moore Cornwall, though he again signed my book with his pseudonym.

The English poet Fleur Adcock said in April 1989, 'Thank you for your note. I don't at all mind signing books, but I hate wrapping parcels! So perhaps you would send them in a jiffy bag which I can use for the return trip, with a new label. (Plus postage, as you propose). I think my writing's worse than yours!' In May 1991 Iris Murdoch wrote, 'Thank you for your kind letter. Yes, do send book – with, if you please, suitable return envelope. I have no secretary, and that would save time! Thank you for writing, and all the best.' In December 1993, Martin Amis said, 'Thank you for your letter and request for my signature. I'm afraid I really cannot cope with stacks of books through the post, and must confess to sometimes leaving them for their full term at the sorting office as I usually seem to be out whenever the post office delivers. If you would like to send sticky labels, I would be delighted to sign them.' And when I asked Paul Theroux to sign *Mosquito Coast* he replied, 'Thanks for your letter. Please don't send me a book, but perhaps you might paste this onto the flyleaf as a memento? Paul Theroux.' Doris Lessing wrote 'I simply do not have time to take parcels to the Post Office – I hope this card will do instead.' And when I asked Peter Shaffer to sign my copy of *Equus* he wrote back on a card, 'May I suggest you paste this card into the book. Simpler than sending the book to New York.' This practice of sending signed stickers is not uncommon. It certainly saves money on postage as well as a lot of bother for the author, but for the collector it is not quite the same as getting the book itself signed. Collectors want to know that the author has actually held and signed their personal copy.

Over the years there were some interesting replies to my requests for signatures. In 1983 after he had signed *My Uncle Oswald,* Roald Dahl wrote, 'Here's your book, signed with pleasure. It was very considerate of you to send the return postage. You would be astonished if you knew how many people didn't.' In 1985 Salman Rushdie replied before I sent him my copies of *Midnight's Children, Shame* and his first book *Grimus* saying 'Thank you for taking the trouble to ask first. Yes I will be happy to sign your books and return them.' (This was before *The Satanic Verses* was published.) In 1987 Richard Gordon wrote 'Delighted to sign the copy of *Doctor in Clover* for you and thank you for your most kind note. How considerate to send postage ... most readers don't.' The playwright Christopher Fry signed my copy of *A Sleep of Prisoners,* and it was later inscribed by Ronald Searle, who had drawn the frontispiece for the book. Again in 1987 P. D. James wrote, 'Many thanks for your letter of 31st January. I am delighted that you have so enjoyed *A Taste for Death,* and shall be happy to sign your copy if you care to send it. I am grateful for your courtesy in asking me first; very few people do!'

In 1988 I wrote to Kingsley Amis and asked if he would sign *Bright November, I Like It Here* and *Lucky Jim* and he replied,

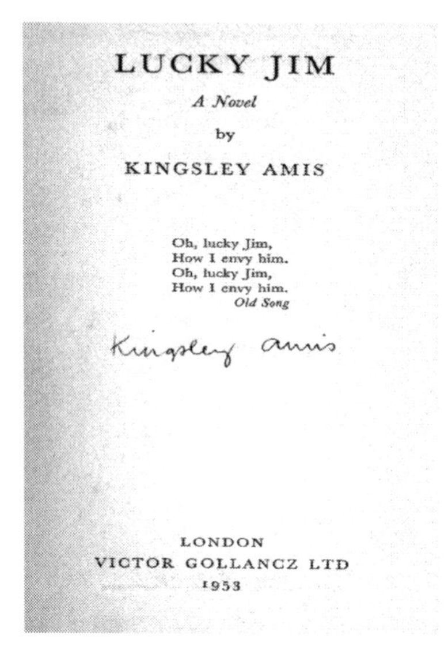
LUCKY JIM

A Novel

by

KINGSLEY AMIS

Oh, lucky Jim,
How I envy him.
Oh, lucky Jim,
How I envy him.
Old Song

Kingsley Amis

LONDON
VICTOR GOLLANCZ LTD
1953

'Thank you for your letter of 30th December. It is most civil of you to ask first whether or not I am prepared to autograph your books. Please send them to me, and I will return as soon as possible.' This was the beginning of a lengthy correspondence with Amis. In another package of books I sent him I enclosed Wendy Cope's *Making Cocoa for Kingsley Amis*. She had already inscribed it and Mr Amis did likewise. And in one of his last letters to me he said, 'Thank you for your letter. You are now an old friend! Please send the books to me, and I will return them as soon as possible. It was kind of you to write. All the best, Yours sincerely, Kingsley Amis.' In 2003 I wrote to the English poet Christopher Middleton to ask him to sign his Turret Broadside *Some Dogs* and he replied, 'How civilised / traditional of you to ask, before sending the text! I praise such archaic gestures. I abominate the impertinence of many contemporary moeurs. But I also abominate the egoism which persuades 'Me', so to praise, so to abominate.' Unknowingly I was taking the right approach, and that may be why so many authors replied to me in such a positive way.

Sometimes authors enclosed another of their books, free, when returning a parcel, and occasionally the postage was returned. A few writers told me that if I wanted books signed again in the future I should just send them and not bother writing for permission. Those who didn't want to sign had the courtesy to reply and give their perfectly valid reasons for not doing so. In 1982 I wrote to Anthony Powell to ask him to sign his sequence of novels *A Dance to the Music of Time* and he replied, 'I am delighted that you like my books, and it was most kind to write. I hope you will not think me ungracious in saying that I cannot sign them, as I have to make a rule that I sign no books for people I have not met personally. This is partly because at moments the business of doing up, etc became too much, partly because I discovered someone was sending me books under various names. I hope that you will forgive the fact that I have to stick to my rule.'

Philip Larkin said, 'Thank you for your letter, but I must explain that for some time now I have tried to maintain the practice of signing only for people known to me. This is because indiscriminate signing seems to devalue copies inscribed to friends, and also because it has not been unknown for such copies to turn up in booksellers' catalogues in a remarkably short space of time. I hope you will understand my reasons for having to decline your request, and sorry not to be more helpful.' An Irish author wrote to say, 'You can get signed copies of my books from Kenny's bookshop in Galway. Sorry I cannot sign or return copies of my books sent to me for signatures.' In January 1988 Timothy Mo replied, 'Thank you for your letter, asking if I would sign your books for you. To be frank, I have no objection to autographing books and have done so many a time at bookshops and lectures; however, the thought of standing in line at the post office to mail the parcel back to you is not at all attractive. I must therefore say that I will not sign the books for you! However, you are now in possession of a signed letter, which is some compensation, I hope.' When I wrote to Francis Stuart in October 1988 he replied, 'I regret not being able to do as you ask. My agent has advised me not to sign any more books as it appears they were being marketed here and in England at exorbitant prices.' Fortunately, when I contacted him again a few years later he did oblige me. I am sure that the practice of selling on signed books often happens without the knowledge of the author or the general public. It is of course a type of fraud and the sad thing is that the people who do this are book people.

Another reaction came from Oliver Reynolds, a Welsh poet with whom I was corresponding in the mid-80s, who also turned out to be a rugby fanatic. When he signed my copies of *Skevington's Daughter* and *The Player Queen's Wife* he asked if I could get a ticket for him for the forthcoming Ireland/Wales rugby match at Lansdowne Road. Welsh rugby was on a high at the time and every man, woman and child in Wales wanted to be in Dublin for the match. Luckily I had access to a ticket and sent it to him. For the record, Ireland won the match and I gained a friend, all in the interests of rugby and literature.

Three more replies: in 1991 Bernard MacLaverty wrote 'Delighted to sign anything except cheques. Just send them on.' John Montague inscribed my copy of *Time in Armagh* 'for Philip Murray – these latest sheafs, instead of medicine bills and prescriptions, with different doses.' And Michael Hartnett said, 'Thank you for buying my book. A poet not only needs an audience, he often needs medical attention as well! Beir Bua agus Beannacht.'

A few writers had difficulty with my handwriting, which didn't surprise me. One wrote, 'I couldn't sign the books to you because of your doctor's signature (Prescriptive). To P. seemed a bit too much', and another wrote 'You have a classical medico hand.' He was obviously trying to be nice to me! Tom Sharpe, regarded as one of the best writers of farce of his generation, had signed for me on several occasions and when I wrote again in 1987 he replied, 'Of course! What on earth do you do with my signed books? Or, perhaps, you are into signed copies futures. The thing is, do you read my books? (2 things in one sentence, alas.) P.S. The chemists in Sligo must be mind-readers to cope with your prescriptions. I thought my handwriting was illegible!' When I wrote to thank him I assured him that I had read all his books and still had space for more signed copies. I also told him that when any of the chemists in Sligo get a prescription they cannot decipher they know immediately it is from me.

I wrote to Graham Greene care of his publisher twice during the seventies, allowing a decent interval between letters, but as I didn't get a reply I felt he might not have received either letter.

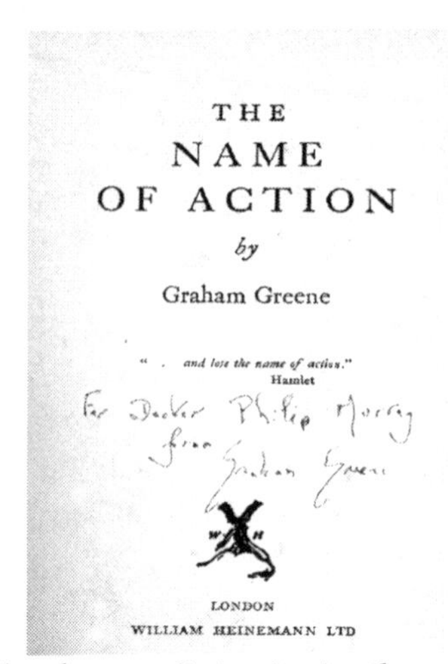

THE
NAME
OF ACTION
by
Graham Greene

"... and lose the name of action."
Hamlet

LONDON
WILLIAM HEINEMANN LTD

In 1980 I learnt that he was living in Antibes so I addressed my letter to 'Mr Graham Greene, Antibes, France'. My persistence paid off. He wrote back: 'Many thanks for your kind complimentary letter. I would be glad to sign a book of yours, but the trouble is that it will cost you a great deal sending it to Antibes and it will cost me a great deal of time standing in a queue to return it. If you would send one book that you like the best to my sister (address enclosed), I will sign it when I am next in England.' I eventually decided to send his second book, *The Name of Action*, which was the earliest of his books that I had. My copy was returned, inscribed to me, about three months after I posted it. What I didn't know until I read his biography years later was that Greene was embarrassed about this book and also by his first book, *The Man Within*, and wanted to distance himself from both of them. Neither book is listed in his bibliography. So I am still astounded that he actually inscribed *The Name of Action* rather than sending it back unsigned. He had the reputation of being a difficult and complex person but this shows his humanity. I suspect that very few other copies of this particular book have been signed.

Some replies were very short. William Golding sent a postcard on which he typed 'O.K. W.G.', but the shortest reply of all came from the American novelist John Barth, who sent a postcard which contained one word: 'Sure.' Golding subsequently signed my copies of his trilogy *Rites of Passage*, *Close Quarters* and

Fire Down Below, and Barth signed my copy of *Giles Goat-Song*.

There was only one cantankerous reply over the years, from the American writer Harold Brodsky after his long-awaited first novel, *The Runaway Soul*, was published in 1991. When I wrote to him I mentioned some of the mixed reviews his book had received on this side of the Atlantic. Perhaps I was too honest in my comments because he took my remarks as open criticism. He wasn't prepared to sign my copy but he sent me a signed sticker to be inserted in the book. He also said, 'I don't think the reviews were generally negative. You don't perhaps read widely enough.' When I wrote to thank him I asked for certain information about *The New Yorker* as he was on its editorial board at the time. He replied, 'You are becoming irritating.' So that was the end of that correspondence.

I greatly admire the work of the Czech writer Milan Kundera and have bought and read everything he has written. He is not what some would call a popular writer but comes across as a very principled man. I wondered what response I would get when I first wrote to him in 1986. His wife Vera replied saying that he would be delighted to sign my books and he duly obliged when I sent him *The Unbearable Lightness of Being* and *Laughable Loves*. In 1997 I asked if he would sign my copies of *The Farewell Party* and his first book, *The Joke*, both of which I had bought and read in the meantime. This time his wife wrote back with a most unusual request: her husband would be deeply grateful if he could keep my copy of *The Joke* (which was a true English first edition). She said that in its place he would send a signed copy of the newly revised edition of the book as well as a signed copy of his latest book, *Immortality*. She went on to explain that even after all these years he was still upset by the original English translation and confiscated any copies he laid his hands on (shades of Patrick White!). Naturally I complied with his request. When the books arrived back from Paris I saw that the author's note in the newly revised edition started as follows: 'If it didn't concern me, it would certainly make me laugh: This is the fifth English-language version of *The Joke*. The first version was published in London in 1969 by Macdonald, in a translation by David Hamblyn and Oliver Stalleybrass. I remember my amazement when I received the book in Prague; I didn't recognise it at all. The novel was entirely reconstructed; divided into a different number of parts, with chapters shortened or simply omitted.' At the end of the note he said 'To my readers, a promise: There will not be a sixth English-language version of *The Joke*.' After reading the revised edition and comparing it with the original English edition I could see that the points he made were completely valid.

Sligo, where I live, has a rich cultural heritage and is known internationally as a major literary and artistic area, originally due to the renown of the Yeats brothers. Today, Sligo and its environs are the home of many well-known writers and artists, including Barrie Cooke, Dermot Healy, Leland Bardwell, Sean McSweeney, Brian Leydon, Patrick Hall, Diarmuid Delargy, Eoin McNamee, Nick Miller and others. The annual Yeats International Summer School, which recently celebrated its fiftieth anniversary, gives the area added status. It holds a pre-eminent place in Ireland's artistic calendar and attracts poets, academics, novelists and students from all over the world. Those who are invited to lecture or give a poetry reading feel privileged to have their involvement on their CV.

I have found that having Sligo, Ireland, as my address when I write to authors all over the world is very much in my favour. Thomas Keneally wrote in 1980, 'It is a wonderful thing to have readers in far places, and the mists of Sligo seem very remote from the humidity of Sydney on a day like this.' Len Deighton wrote in 1983, 'I've been on a long trip and your letter was waiting for me when I returned here two days ago. Thank you for writing. I'm sure there's no need to tell you how much any writer enjoys hearing from a reader, and it's especially good to hear from a fellow countryman.' Richard Gordon of *Doctor in the House* fame wrote in 1984, 'I am sad never to have visited Sligo, though I believe I am the only English doctor ever to have delivered a lecture on gout in Cork.' Kathleen Raine inscribed her book *On a Deserted Shore*, 'Signed for Philip Murray, in Sligo, of so many happy memories. February 1987.' In 1984 James Michener wrote, 'It is a pleasure to send the enclosed signed card to Sligo and Ireland, a land whose beauty lives in my memory.' John Osborne wrote, 'Thank you for your note. Of course I will sign your copy of *Look Back in Anger*. It's rather nice to see Sligo, Ireland, rather than Éire.' In June 1987 Robertson Davies wrote, 'Many thanks for your letter which has just reached me, having been sent on by British Penguin. I should be delighted to autograph one of your books if you will send it to me and am very happy indeed to hear from a reader in Ireland.' Robertson Davies is regarded by many as the greatest Canadian writer ever and the book I sent him to sign was *What's Bred in the Bone*.

In 1988 after Paul Auster signed his trilogy *The Locked Room, Ghosts* and *City of Glass* he wrote saying, 'I spent some time in Sligo many years ago (1972), and have fond memories of the place.' In 1993 the legendary Kurt Vonnegut wrote, 'What an honour to receive such a request from a nation which has made such stunning contributions to literature. If you will tell me which book of mine you would like me to autograph, I will send you a copy from here.' We got our wires crossed however and I never did get a book from him but what a wonderful letter. In 1989 Colin Wilson wrote, 'Yes, by all means send *The Outsider* for signature – it would be helpful if you would enclose a bookbag with your address on it. We were in Sligo many years ago just after *The Outsider* came out, and I still remember it with great nostalgia.'

In the early nineties I wrote to the crime writer James Lee Burke asking him to sign my copies of *Cimarron Rose* and *In the Electric Mist with Confederate Dead* and he said, 'Thanks for your nice letter. It's better not to send books for me to sign. I use three addresses, and travel all over, and the books stand a good chance of being lost or rained upon. I hope to meet you in Ireland. Thank you for your kind remarks about my books. All the best.' He hasn't turned up yet but there's plenty of time. Many other letters were in a similar vein and though many foreigners still see Ireland through green-tinted glasses, there is a genuine depth of feeling towards our country, and an appreciation of its literature.

Over the years I have had some amusing inscriptions, particularly those of Julian Barnes, who between 1980 and 1987 wrote four detective books under the pseudonym Dan Kavanagh. The hero in this series is Duffy, a popular bisexual sleuth. On the dust jacket of *Duffy*, the first book in the series, the author wrote the following blurb, very much tongue-in-cheek: 'Dan Kavanagh was born in County Sligo in 1946. Having devoted his adolescence to truancy, venery, and petty theft, he left home at seventeen and signed on as a deckhand on a Liberian tanker. After jumping ship at Montevideo, he roamed across the Americas taking a variety of jobs. He was a steer-wrestler, a waiter on roller-skates at a drive-in eatery in Tucson, and a bouncer in a gay bar in San Francisco. He is currently working in London and lives in North Islington.' The blurbs on the other three detective books were in a similar vein.

Barnes had signed books for me on several occasions and agreed to do so again when I contacted him in the mid-eighties and sent him several books written under his own name as well as the Duffy book. When the books were returned *Duffy* was inscribed: 'Once treated by Dr Murray of the Sligo Medicentre for an unmentionable disease – Dan Kavanagh.' In September 2006 he was one of the authors invited to read at Scríobh, the Sligo Literary Festival. Afterwards I showed him my copy of *Duffy*, which he remembered inscribing. He then inscribed *Love, Etc*, the latest book under his own name, 'To Philip that word-doctor of Sligo from Julian Barnes – who unlike Dan Kavanagh has never been treated by him.' His third Dan Kavanagh book, *Putting the Boot In*, was later signed 'Dan Kavanagh, that Sligo boy', and a card followed saying 'Sorry, Dan's handwriting hasn't improved. Must have been that Sligo schooling.' I hope Mr Barnes had as much fun writing these inscriptions as I had reading them.

Another writer of supposed Sligo ancestry is the Goon, Spike Milligan. On the wall of a house in Holborn Street in the middle of Sligo a plaque states that this was the residence of Spike's father Leo and his grandfather Sergeant William Miller. The plaque reads, 'My father was born in Sligo – very Irish, very working class family, very poor.' Spike Milligan's great book *Puckoon* was published in 1963 and is often described as a book of comedy and disaster. He agreed to sign my copy and returned it with the inscription 'Spike Milligan 1803.' I still haven't figured out what that date is supposed to mean. A letter enclosed with the book said, 'Dear Philip, enclosed is your book which I have signed. Thanks for sending the postage. I must tell you it's a very, very rare occasion that happens – Love, Light, and Peace – Spike.'

On 29 August 2003 I received a letter from Lawrence Ferlinghetti. This happened about six months after earlier correspondence when he had signed his Turret Press broadside, *Spirit of the Crusades,* for me. His letter read, 'I am wondering if, among your Irish literary contacts, you have any connection with anyone directing an Irish poetry festival annually or semi-annually. That is, of the kind that invites foreign authors. I have not been in Ireland since the time I was practically penniless in Dublin as a student in about 1949, having been on vacation from the University of Paris where I was working on a doctorate. (I was in Northern Ireland on a US subchaser during world war two.) But I've been wanting to return for a visit all these years and have never made it back. If you could wangle an invitation, with some accommodation, I would come! Any leads you could give me would be a great help.' This was too good an opportunity to pass up so I immediately phoned local writers Dermot Healy and Leland Bardwell and the directors of the Model Arts Centre in Sligo. They were excited about my proposition and all agreed that I could invite Ferlinghetti to give a reading sometime the following June.

Ferlinghetti was eighty-five years of age at the time and was accompanied on his trip by the internationally renowned photographer and film-maker Chris Felver. For a man of his age Ferlinghetti was very sprightly and extremely alert. He later told me that he swam every day as well as cycling to and from work at his City Lights Bookstore. The shop is on Columbus Avenue in the North Beach area of San Francisco and is one of the most famous bookshops in the world. Unfortunately, it is also one of the dwindling number of independent bookshops in America. A street very close to City Lights is named after Ferlinghetti and in 1998 he was declared the first poet laureate of San Francisco. He appears to have come through unscathed from the heady days of Beat poetry when he spent much time with Allen Ginsberg, Gregory Corso, Jack Kerouac, Michael McClure, William Burroughs, Diane Di Prima, Anne Waldman, Gary Snyder and Neal Cassidy. Ferlinghetti is still writing: *Americus 1,* his most recent book of poetry, is the first in a new series of five books.

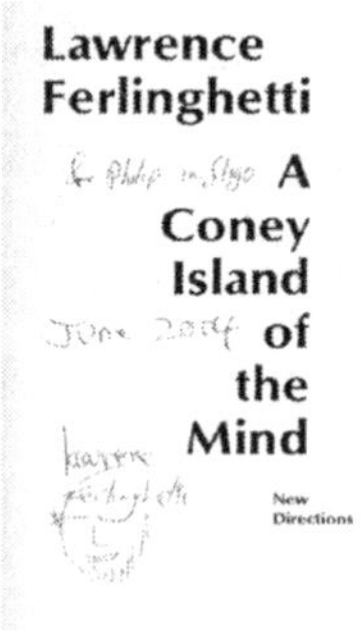

About six weeks before the reading in Sligo, Ferlinghetti e-mailed me to say that the director of the Dublin Writers Festival, the poet Pat Boran, wanted him to read during that festival. This presented a problem as the date clashed with the Sligo event. I encouraged him to read in Dublin but said that his first ever reading in Ireland simply had to be in Sligo. He agreed to that so we rearranged the Sligo reading to take place four days before the Dublin event. The Model Arts Centre was packed on the night of the reading. What pleased Ferlinghetti most was the number of young people in the audience, which shows the timelessness of his poetry. He read mostly from his great book *A Coney Island of the Mind* and the consensus afterwards was that it had been a very special night and one of the best readings anyone had ever attended. Afterwards we retired to Connolly's pub, where he sat on a *sugán* chair drinking Guinness, talking to everyone and signing books for those who wanted. He was very much at ease and very complimentary about the ambience of Connolly's.

The next day we went to Yeats' grave in Drumcliffe churchyard. This was something of a pilgrimage for Ferlinghetti, as he is a devotee of the great man and his writing is full of Yeatsian references. In the churchyard he sat on a tombstone for about half an hour, quietly contemplating the world. I thought he was taking notes but instead he wrote the following poem and later gave me the manuscript:

That Golden Bird

That Golden Bird

That spreads its wings

Beyond the dark landscape
And Sings and Sings
And sings pure lyric threnodies

Aye Golden Bird
Whose name I never can remember
O drunk flute
Singing flower
Distant
Hidden
Lonely
Echoing
In the twilight
In the gloaming
I hear her again
In Sligo
Sweet soul singer
Bird of flight
May I hear you ever
Singing to me solo
In dead of night.

Lawrence Ferlinghetti 8/6/04

On Ferlinghetti's last day in Sligo we went to Coney Island, courtesy of local boatman Darrel Ewing, and this proved to be the highlight of his trip. The single pub on the island is owned by John McGowan, who opened up especially for the occasion. While sitting in the bar drinking his Guinness Ferlinghetti inscribed my copy of *A Coney Island of the Mind* as follows: 'For Philip Murray on (the original) Coney Island 2004. Are we having a pint together in that three hundred year old pub where they locked the doors during holy hour which meant, you couldn't git out. Love and Kisses, Lawrence Ferlinghetti.' Chris Felver and he travelled to Dublin the next day for his reading at the Writers' Festival and later in the week went on to Berlin for the Poetry Festival there. Ferlinghetti was the main attraction at both events and read to full houses.

When Ferlinghetti set out for Sligo he had three main objectives: to give his first ever reading in Ireland, to visit Yeats' grave, and to go to Coney Island, all of which he achieved. He later told me that the three days spent in Sligo were the high point of the entire trip, and that included his time in both Dublin and Berlin. He also said that he felt so much at home in Sligo he was toying with the idea of taking a cottage for a month to do some writing, but this hasn't materialised. The arts editor of the *Sligo Champion* wrote at the end of 2004 that Ferlinghetti's reading had been the major event of the year. He is certainly one of the most extraordinary men I have ever met. In 2008 Gavin Newsom, the mayor of San Francisco, declared that 24 March, Ferlinghetti's birthday, would henceforth be called Lawrence Ferlinghetti Day in honour of what he has done for the city. This is an extraordinary achievement in his own lifetime, especially as he had already had a street named after him. It is good to be able to say that even with all these accolades he appears not to have changed in the slightest. Having attended the truly great reading by Ferlinghetti in Sligo I was reminded of what was once said about readings:

> 'No matter what degree of pleasure
> You give an audience, there is no greater
> Pleasure thereafter than the pleasure
> You give them when you shut up.'

Needless to say, the above lines did not apply to Ferlinghetti's reading.

In spring 1990 Vivien and I went on one of our trips to Australia and as usual I spent a few days touring the Sydney bookshops. One of these, in the eastern suburbs, was owned by an old friend, James Larsen. On the day I went there he was reading a paperback copy of *Blood Meridian* by Cormac McCarthy and suggested that I should read it too. I hadn't heard of the author before and presumed that with a first name like Cormac and a surname like McCarthy he had to be Irish, but James told me he was an American. Back in Ireland I discovered that McCarthy's books were not available at the time in either hardback or paperback. A short while later *Blood Meridian* turned up in an American catalogue and I bought it. The copy was a first American edition, in immaculate condition, with a dust jacket, and it cost me twenty-five American dollars. Very

Cormac McCarthy

BLOOD MERIDIAN

or The Evening Redness in the West

PICADOR

published by Pan Books

few books, if any, have had such a profound effect on me. I couldn't put it down and it is one of the best books I have ever read. I immediately set out to buy the other four novels that had appeared by then: *The Orchard Keeper, Outer Dark, Child of God* and *Suttree.* Over the next few months they each turned up in American catalogues and I was able to get them for between twenty and thirty dollars each.

I spoke enthusiastically about McCarthy's books to reader and writer friends and was surprised to learn that not only had they not read him but most had never heard of him. John McGahern was the one exception and he was full of praise. After I had read the five books I wrote to McCarthy through his then publishers, Random House, and he kindly agreed to sign my copies for me. When I wrote to him I suggested that he must have some Irish blood in him. He told me that that was the case but that his family had been unable to trace their Irish roots. It still amazes me that he was ignored by the American literary critics as well as the American reading public for so many years. At this stage I decided to embark on what was to become my fourth complete author collection, despite the fact that McCarthy was then practically unknown. I was fascinated by his writing.

McCarthy's break-through novel *All the Pretty Horses* was published in 1992. It won both the National Book Award and the National Book Critics Award in America, finally giving him the recognition he was due. *All the Pretty Horses* was followed by the two other volumes of the Border Trilogy, *The Crossing* and *Cities of the Plain*, both published to huge acclaim. Suddenly McCarthy's books were being collected like never before. Since then *No Country for Old Men* and *The Road* have been published and both have been filmed. There is a lot of controversy over the perceived violence in these two books: a close friend of mine cannot contemplate even opening either of them. The violence, though, is a necessary part of the story and is not there just for the sake of violence.

It is less well known that McCarthy has published three plays: *Stonemason, The Gardener's Son* and *The Sunset Limited*. The last of these was performed at the 2007 Galway Arts Festival by the Chicago-based Steppenwolf Theatre Company, with the original cast on stage. I had the great pleasure of attending the performance.

Fewer than fifteen thousand copies in total are said to have been published in first edition for McCarthy's first five books. However, with the success of *All the Pretty Horses* in 1992 his books are now published in print runs of over one hundred thousand copies for the first edition. The first five books have been reprinted many times in the interim, but the true first American editions of these books remain very scarce and are of course collectors' items. All the books have been translated into many different languages.

When I started checking up on McCarthy's contributions to literary journals etc, I found that there weren't many. His first two publications were short stories that appeared in the literary supplement of the University of Tennessee magazine *The Phoenix*. The first was entitled *Wake for Susan* and appeared in the October 1959 issue; the second, *A Drowning Incident*, appeared in the March 1960 issue. I have not been able to buy or even see copies of these. Another five journal contributions consist of excerpts from his novels: *Bounty from The Orchard Keeper* in the *Yale Review* in 1965, *The Dark Waters from The Orchard Keeper* in the *Sewanee Review* in 1965, *Burial from Suttree* in *Antaeus* in 1979, *The Scalphunters from Blood Meridian* in *TriQuarterly* in 1980, and an extract from *All the Pretty Horses* in *Esquire* in 1992. These journals are still available so a new McCarthy collector would not find collecting his work difficult once the first five novels have been obtained. I simply bought each book at the published price as it came out.

A little-known McCarthy item is a poster *Already You Could See Through the Dust on the Ponies Hides*. This poster contains a 220 word excerpt from *Blood Meridian* and measures 34 x 24 inches. It was published in May 2000 in a one-off issue of 400 copies to coincide with McCarthy becoming Texan Writer of the Year. In the intervening years I had never seen a copy, nor had any dealer I spoke to heard of it. True to form, Jim O Halloran tracked down a copy last year. He bought it in a Texas bookshop and paid 55 dollars. McCarthy has also written several screenplays and countless drafts.

Many American critics describe McCarthy as a recluse and place him in the same category as J. D. Salinger and Thomas Pynchon. I think this is because he has never given a reading and had only given two interviews until *The Road* was picked as a selection for Oprah Winfrey's Book Club. He then gave a televised interview to the talk show diva and put himself firmly in the public eye. Other interviews followed in major periodicals such as *Rolling Stone* and *The Wall Street Journal*. To describe McCarthy as a recluse in the manner of Salinger or Pynchon is inaccurate. I know nothing of Pynchon's situation but Salinger was apparently alarmed by his sudden fame after the publication of *Catcher in the Rye* in 1951. He went into voluntary hiding and was rarely seen right up to the time of his recent death. McCarthy isn't a recluse: when he visited Sligo I realised he was simply a very private person, though he was happy to take part in the delights of Connolly's pub.

The *New York Times* reported in December 2009 that McCarthy had offered his portable Olivetti manual typewriter for auction, with the proceeds to be donated to the Santa Fe Institute, to which he is attached. He told the *Times* reporter that he had typed five million words on the machine and Christie's estimated that it would fetch between $15,000 and $20,000. In fact it realised a quarter of a million dollars.

For many, *Suttree* is McCarthy's greatest book, and more recently *The Road* has been described as his masterpiece. For me *Blood Meridian* is his greatest book, and not just because it was the first one I read. For a long time it was one of the most unread masterpieces of American fiction but in a survey conducted by the *New York Times Book Review* recently it was voted one of the five best books of the last quarter century. He should certainly win the Nobel Prize: his writing deserves as much and he is now regarded as the author all American writers have to measure themselves against. For me, collecting Cormac McCarthy is still a work in progress, as I feel certain there is more to come. I should say that when I first contacted him in the early nineties he was virtually unknown either in America or abroad. I wrote to him simply because I admired his writing.

Although I have sent books to every corner of the world it is good to report that in forty years only one book has been lost, or rather misappropriated. This was *Death of a Salesman* which happened to be the only book of Arthur Miller's that I possessed. After the Abbey Theatre's production of the play in 1986, with Ray McAnally starring as Willy Loman, I wrote to ask if Miller would sign my copy. It proved very difficult to get his address but eventually I wrote to him care of Temple University, Philadelphia. He replied 'I am in receipt of your letter of 30th January, with the inquiry regarding a signature in your book. If you will send me the copy of the book which you purchased, I shall of course be pleased to sign it – Arthur Miller.' So I sent the book to the same address, as usual enclosing return postage. That was the last I heard of my copy, in spite of several letters of enquiry sent over the following six months. It then dawned on me that I might have written to the wrong Arthur Miller, so I bought another copy and started again. This time I found the right man, and in my letter to him related the above saga as well as enclosing a copy of the first Arthur Miller's letter. When my book came back Miller had enclosed the copy of that letter.

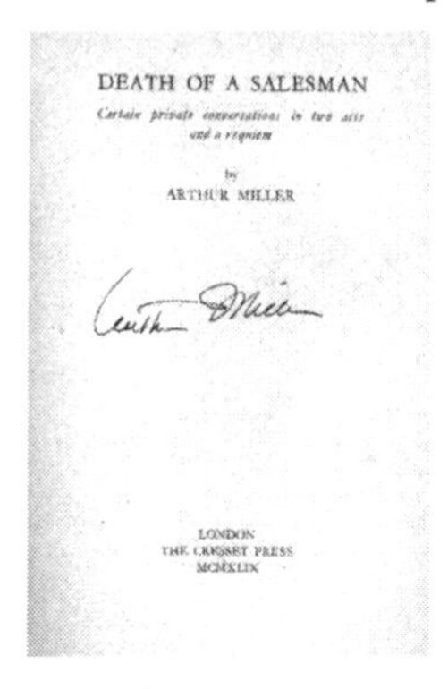
DEATH OF A SALESMAN

Certain private conversations in two acts and a requiem

by

ARTHUR MILLER

LONDON
THE CRESSET PRESS
MCMXLIX

On it he had drawn an arrow pointing to the first Arthur Miller's signature and written beside it 'Wrong Man'. Another arrow pointed to his own signature and beside that he wrote 'Right man. But he must have your book because I don't – Arthur Miller.' Obviously I was conned by the first Mr Miller who I suspect was, unfortunately, a fellow medic. But at least I got an inscribed copy.

The minimal loss of books says a lot for the postal systems of the world, though there were two near misses. One of these concerned Bruce Chatwin's *In Patagonia*. After I had sent it, with his permission to do so, I heard nothing for nearly six months. I wasn't unduly concerned as I had sent books to him before and knew he was reliable and that he travelled extensively, often for long periods of time. Out of the blue one day the postman delivered a large plastic sack containing my book and a letter of explanation from the post office. It seemed that a cargo ship had sunk in port but that the entire contents, including my book, had been salvaged. The book had, though, been completely destroyed by sea water and was unreadable, so I threw it out. Chatwin signed my copies of *Songlines*, perhaps his best book, and *The Viceroy of Ouidah* before his untimely death in 1989. I never told him about the saga with *In Patagonia*.

The other near miss occurred when I wrote to the Colombian Nobel Prize winning writer Gabriel Garcia Marquez in 1989. Like my experience of writing to Beckett some years earlier, I was uncertain about doing this and dithered for quite a while before finally plucking up my courage. I was aware that he rarely signed books for anyone, and never for American citizens. In March 1989 his secretary wrote from Mexico City saying 'Dear Dr Murray, Senor Garcia Marquez with much pleasure will sign the books you may wish to send.' I had heard that the Mexican postal system is one of the most unreliable anywhere in the world but I decided to chance it and sent eleven books, including a first American edition of his masterpiece, *A Hundred Years of Solitude*. The books were carefully packed in a cardboard box and return postage was enclosed but nearly a year went by without any further word. I was certain my luck had run out and I would never see my copies again. But then my reliable postman delivered another sealed plastic sack with all eleven books inside. This time the post office explained that the return package had burst open and had had to be repacked. All the books were inscribed and the author had drawn various images in some of them, so it was worth the wait.

In the early nineties I was asked by a friend in Dublin if I would look after the Canadian writer Douglas Coupland when he visited Sligo. The only thing I knew about him before we met in Connolly's was that he had written *Generation X: Tales for an Accelerated Culture*. We spent a few hours chatting about literature and I found him a pleasant man. He told me that the main reason for his visit was to research a book he was planning to write about Ireland, which he hoped would turn out to be the great Irish novel. Before we parted that evening he gave me a presentation copy of *Generation X*, though he said he thought I wouldn't enjoy it. He also asked me to write to him after I had read it and tell him whether I thought he could write the great Irish novel. He was right: I didn't enjoy the book, which meant nothing to me, and his writing seemed to be from another planet. When I wrote to him I decided to be honest and in effect said that on the evidence of *Generation X* I didn't feel he was qualified to write a great Irish novel. *Generation X* went on to become an international bestseller. Coupland became a millionaire and the term itself, like Joseph Heller's *Catch 22*, entered the vernacular. He has gone on to write more than twenty-five fiction and non-fiction books with such titles as *Shampoo Planet*, *Girlfriend in a Coma* and *All Families are Psychotic*, with the latest being *Generation A*. The books have exotic titles but I have refrained from either reading or buying them. He never did write the great Irish novel, nor did he ever reply to my letter.

Les Murray is regarded as one of the outstanding poets of his generation, as well as being one of Australia's most influential literary critics. He has published about thirty volumes of poetry and is sometimes spoken of as a possible Nobel Prize winner. He has for many years been one of my favourite poets and I have quite a number of his books, including *The Ilex Tree*, *Selected Poems*, *The Boys Who Stole the Funeral*, *The Daylight Moon*, *Dog Fox Field* and *Subhuman Redneck Poems*. We have corresponded quite a bit over the years and he signed all my copies for me. In a letter in November 1988 he said, 'What a pity we two

Murrays didn't get to meet.' This was rectified in the early nineties when he gave a poetry reading at the Yeats Memorial Building in Sligo. It was my great pleasure to look after him and show him round the area next day, including the inevitable pilgrimage to Yeats' grave. It was his first visit to Sligo and he was most impressed. Our relationship was cemented as a result of this meeting. Before he left Sligo that day he inscribed his *Collected Poems* 'For my clansman Philip, and my compatriot Vivien, with warm regards – Les. Sligo 15/6/02', and he also inscribed *Equanimities* as follows: 'Philip – of course you know the Scottish Murray prayer: Lord, gies a guid conceit o' ourselves – Best wishes, Les Murray.'

Over the years I have learned that some authors, although willing to sign, will not sign certain of their books. Of course they are not obliged to say why but both Patrick White and Milan Kundera explained why they didn't want to sign particular books. Usually such books are the first ones authors publish and they may be embarrassed about the quality of writing. Graham Greene seemed to break his own rule when he signed *The Name of Action* for me. William Trevor had signed books for me on several occasions so I was surprised when a box of books I had sent him was returned with one of the titles unsigned. This was his first book, *A Standard of Behaviour,* and I later found out that he never signed this book for anyone. If I had known this in advance, of course I wouldn't have sent it. Trevor continues to be very generous to me but this title has never been mentioned again.

All book collectors make a point of visiting secondhand bookshops. We all have a list in our heads of books that we are searching for and we are always looking out for a bargain in whatever field. Hope springs eternal! As well as in secondhand bookshops bargains can be found in the strangest of places, including junk shops, charity shops, house auctions and secondhand furniture stores as well as at formal book auctions. House auctions can be a disappointment because as often as not the auctioneer will have allowed a book dealer friend to look over the contents before the day of sale and naturally he or she will have taken the best items. Auctions have never appealed to me and I have only attended a few charity events.

In 1995, while attending a meeting in Brussels, I spent an afternoon scouting the secondhand bookshops. Nearly all the books were in French, Flemish or German but in one shop there was a single shelf with about twenty books in English. In their midst was a first English edition of John Fowles' *The French Lieutenant's Woman,* which I knew was worth about £50 at the time. It was a good clean copy in a dust jacket and it cost me £3. On another occasion I found a copy of William Boyd's first novel, *A Good Man in Africa,* in a secondhand furniture shop in Sligo. It was a first English edition in immaculate condition and I paid 50 pence for it. Today it sells for €300 or more. Again in Sligo, about thirty years ago, there was a rare book fair that had been heavily advertised and was attended by book dealers and collectors from all over the country. After about an hour there I realised that over ninety per cent of the books on offer were on either history or topography, which were of little interest to me. However, while checking through a few boxes of books of various kinds I found an American first edition of Joseph Heller's most famous book, *Catch 22.* Unfortunately, it didn't have a dust jacket but as it cost me just £1 I couldn't complain. Some time later I wrote to Heller to ask if he would sign it for me but I never heard anything from him. Today the book is worth hundreds of euro.

One of my most memorable finds was in the mid-seventies when I was browsing in Webb's secondhand bookshop on the quays in Dublin and found a copy of Anthony Burgess's *A Clockwork Orange*. It was a first English edition, with a dust jacket, for which I paid £1, knowing it to be worth then about £150. Burgess was internationally famous at the time, mainly because of this book and because of the film based on it that was first screened in 1971. What surprised me was that other scavengers like myself hadn't picked it up before me, but perhaps it had only been put on the shelf that morning.

Two years ago, again while browsing in Dublin's bookshops, I picked up a first American edition of Colum McCann's first book, *Songdogs,* for €8. This was the true first edition and is today worth €150. My most recent discovery happened in Cyprus when I spotted a few shelves of secondhand books in a supermarket, of all places. The books were mainly paperbacks in various languages, all on sale for €3 each. In their midst I found a first English edition of Marilynne Robinson's third book, *Home*. It had a dust jacket and was in mint condition. After I had read it, I checked the title on the internet and found that the cheapest copy was selling for €60. None of the titles mentioned in these three paragraphs had been on my wants list, and apart from *Catch 22* and *Home* I already had copies of the rest. Money was not an issue in these searches, but rather the thrill of the chase and I suppose also the sense of beating the dealer. Unfortunately, such finds are becoming less likely to happen. Nowadays, when a dealer buys a collection that includes books he is unfamiliar with, he has only to check the internet for a valuation and then sell on any copies he doesn't want to specialist dealers.

I obviously took chances by sending books to some of the places that I did, and it is extraordinary that I didn't suffer major losses along the way. It is also worth mentioning the courtesy and generosity I experienced, whether an author was willing to sign or not. Writing to all these authors and sometimes meeting them and becoming friends with them has been great fun for me.

CHAPTER SIX

The Signing of The Whoseday Book

The Whoseday Book was first brought to my attention in March 1999 by John Boland in his Saturday column in *The Irish Times*. He described it as a unique diary for the millennium: it was to be a fund-raising project in aid of The Irish Hospice Foundation, featuring personal contributions from Ireland's leading writers, designers, poets, artists, songwriters, philosophers, composers, musicians, politicians, film-makers and personalities on each page of a very special publication. The organising committee for the project had started work in 1996 under Marie Donnelly, then chair of The Irish Hospice Foundation. The other committee members were John Waters, Eileen Pearson, Colm Tóibín, Perry Ogden, Ciarán Ó Gaora, Marion Cody, Caroline Kennedy and Niamh Sheeran. Apparently a lot of people who heard of the idea of a diary as a fund-raising project were very sceptical. One person said, 'Diaries are ten a penny. Most in fact are given out as freebies by everybody from drug companies to local authorities.'

Eileen Pearson was project manager and later said, 'Almost everyone involved in the creation, publication and marketing of the book gave of their time for little or no fee. Even the contributors themselves would have done anything to help out.' Seamus Heaney agreed to become patron, and as well as writing the introduction he contributed the poem 'Hygeia', written especially for the publication. Heaney's hands were photographed by another contributor, Perry Ogden, and this image became the frontispiece of the book.

In the first instance, the committee drew up a list of 1000 names for possible inclusion. After much debate this was reduced to 366, one for each day of the leap year 2000. The people selected were Irish or Irish at heart, and the final selection was based on gender balance and having a good mix of writers, artists, politicians, etc. About 40 of the potential contributors were born outside Ireland, including Jean Kennedy-Smith, J. P. Donleavy, John Montague and George Mitchell in America, Kevin Volans in South Africa, Sonja Landweer in Holland, Martyn Turner, Barrie Cooke, Marianne Faithful and Hughie O'Donoghue in England, Leland Bardwell in India, John Rocha in Hong Kong, Julie Parsons and Hammon Journeaux in New Zealand, Elizabeth Magill in Canada, Sibylle Ungers in Germany, and Francis Stuart and Jacqueline O'Brien in Australia. Many of these were born of Irish parents, and most came to live in Ireland and are still here. Those chosen were invited to contribute whatever they wished. They were told they wouldn't be able to claim a particular date in the book and that their contribution should take up no more than one page. Playwright Martin McDonagh managed to squeeze a 500-word play, *The Tale of the Town on the River*, onto his page, which was an achievement in itself.

The original idea for the book had come from *The Irish Times* columnist and author John Waters, who also suggested the title. He described it as 'An anthology-cum-millennium-cum-diary-cum-thought-for-the-day prayerbook', and later said that it was 'A representation of the collective mood in Ireland at this moment in time, to be savoured, of course, on the allotted days in the year 2000, but also beyond, in times when the formal record of our time will provide mostly mysteries.' Two-and-a-half years of planning were needed to bring the book to fruition. The Allied Irish Bank Group was a fund-raising partner, which allowed all profits to go to The Irish Hospice Foundation. The bank's CEO, Lochlann Quinn, who is a patron of the arts, wrote the foreword and Marie Donnelly, the editor of the book, wrote a further introduction on behalf of The Irish Hospice Foundation.

When I made enquiries about buying a copy of *The Whoseday Book* I was informed that it wasn't yet available in general bookshops and could only be bought direct from the Foundation's head office in Dublin. It cost £30 and when my copy arrived in April 1999 I was most impressed. It was beautifully produced with Irish linen-covered boards and was printed on art paper, with an image and text on each page. It came with both a dust wrapper and a slip case.

I then decided to buy a second copy and try to repeat what I had done with *Soft Day* (Chapter 2): get all the contributors to sign on the page they had contributed. As I was now an experienced autograph hunter, I realised that this was going to prove a much greater challenge than my earlier effort, if for no other reason than the numbers involved: 366 in *The Whoseday Book* against 36 in *Soft Day*. Also, I had never heard of a lot of the contributors and many of them lived abroad. Another difficulty was that many contributors were ex-directory and could only be contacted via their agents. It would never, of course, be possible to get the entire complement to sign the book as four of the contributors – the painter Patrick Hickey, the Northern Ireland politician Paddy Devlin and the writers Iris Murdoch and Brian Moore – had died before publication. The writer Leland Bardwell later said to me, very much tongue-in-cheek, that a séance would have to be held to get these four signatures. Despite these difficulties, I felt when I started out that to get 200 signatures would be a realistic target, with 250 a possibility and 300 the ultimate aim. Why did I embark on such a venture? I can only say that it presented a challenge and that I looked forward to it. It was to prove my most ambitious project in the world of books and in every way an epic journey.

My first effort was on Monday 19 April 1999, when Vivien and I went to the Galway literary festival, Cúirt, where Dervla Murphy was giving a rare interview to Lelia Doolan, followed on the same programme by Benedict Kiely giving a prose reading. Galway's town hall was packed for the occasion. Afterwards I met all three contributors, none of whom had yet seen the book. They were very impressed with its quality as well as being interested in seeing their own contributions. Lelia Doolan became the first to sign, as she noted on her page. The other two followed suit and my project was up and running.

Around this time I had arranged to send books to William Trevor so I included my copy of *The Whoseday Book*. After signing he returned it and my other books promptly. This was the first of many times I would commit the copy to the post. Of course I didn't need to use the post for the contributors who live in or near Sligo and over the next few months the artists Barrie Cooke, Ronnie Hughes, Sean McSweeney and Dermot Seymour and the writers Eoin McNamee and John McGahern signed. During the following summers and autumns I attended a lot of literary festivals along the western seaboard and obtained more signatures. At the George Moore Literary Festival in Claremorris I met writers Anthony Cronin, Leland Bardwell, Colm Tóibin, Pat O'Brien, Mary O'Malley, Paul Durcan, Dermot Healy and the painter Michael Kane. Apparently Francis Stuart was booked to give a reading on the day but wasn't well enough to travel. All of these signed or inscribed their respective pages. A few weeks after the Claremorris event I attended the General Humbert School in Ballina mainly to try to meet John Hume, who was giving the keynote address. When I caught up with him afterwards he was very welcoming and wrote, 'For Philip Murray with my very best wishes. Let us now hope that in the new century, we will have the new Ireland. John Hume.'

At the Boyle Arts Festival John Waters gave a long talk on the genesis of the book, but when he was asked about the selection process he refused to comment. Like any such list, a case for the inclusion of many other people could easily be made and I am sure that many who missed out were deeply disappointed. The contributors included quite a few politicians from both North and South of the country but none from the Unionist party, and again Waters refused to say anything about this. He later inscribed my copy from both himself and his daughter.

Quite a few contributors signed at the Scríobh Festival in Sligo in autumn 1999, including writers Michael Longley, John Arden and Margaretta Darcy and playwright Vincent Woods. The Fortieth Yeats International Summer School in Sligo that year was formally opened by Seamus Heaney. He also gave a reading in the Hawkswell theatre, and when I met him afterwards, he inscribed my book as follows:

For Philip
Priest of the Healing
God, Devotee of
Hygeia and Janitor
Of the Unawakening door –
Health and Long Life
Seamus 1 August 1999 in Sligo

The poet Tom Paulin and the historian Roy Foster were also at the Summer School and signed for me that year. John Montague gave a reading during the second week of the school but when I met him in Connolly's pub afterwards he was most reluctant to sign, though he had often signed books for me in the past. After some cajoling he finally agreed but made it quite clear that he was signing under protest. His inscription was as follows:

How sad to be
Cut in half;
And your friend,
(So called)
Doesn't recognise
The Butchery!
I sign, reluctantly
For a Tipperary Fuk..r,
Who should know better!
John.

The reason for his reluctance became apparent later when he stated that 'Paths', the poem he submitted for publication, had been printed with the third verse missing and was therefore meaningless. Some people who later signed the book were offended by the second last line of his inscription but I think it adds a touch of colour. I felt in no way offended but I got the impression when he was leaving Connolly's that night that he wouldn't sign too many more copies. When I met the writer Shane Connaughton at a later time, again in Connolly's, he told me that he had a similar experience to Montague, as his poem 'Stoneface' also had a verse missing when published. He signed on his page and simply remarked on the missing verse. Marie Donnelly, the *Whoseday* chairperson, subsequently denied that there were any verses missing in either poem.

In late August 2000 a once-off literary festival took place in Inishmore, the main Aran Island. The event was American-sponsored and had a prestigious line-up of writers, including Frank McCourt, Edna O'Brien, Cathal Ó Searcaigh, Roddy Doyle and Nuala Ní Dhomhnaill. I was unable to go to Inishmore but my friend Joe Burgess, who was also collecting signatures for *The Whoseday Book,* went for the day. By all accounts it was a unique occasion, and the fact that the general public and the participating writers had to travel on the same ferry to Inishmore added another dimension to it. Joe met all the participating writers during the day and got them to sign both our copies.

Local elections in Ireland took place in summer 2000 and both the Taoiseach, Bertie Ahern, and the Sinn Féin leader, Gerry Adams, were canvassing in Sligo at different times. A friend took the book to the Taoiseach to sign, and another friend arranged for me to meet Gerry Adams in a local hotel, where we had a conversation in Irish before he inscribed the book, again in Irish. Many other contributors signed it in Irish, including Tom MacIntyre, Cathal Ó Searcaigh, Nuala Ní Dhomhnaill, T. K. Whittaker, Biddy Jenkinson, Michael Davitt, Angela Bourke, Liam Ó Muirthile, songwriter Tadhg Mac Donnagáin and uileann piper Ronan Brown. The painter Richard Gorman lives in Italy but was in Dublin for an exhibition when I caught up with him, and he signed the book 'Buonharoro! Best wishes, Richard Gorman. Hanging the nine paintings exhibition. 4th September 2001.' The poet Eiléan Ní Chuilleanáin wrote the following inscription in Latin:

Haec requies mea in
Saeculum Saeculi, hic Habitabo,
Quoniam praeelegi eam.
Ps CXXXI, 13.

The official Irish launch of the book took place in the library of the Royal Dublin Society on Sunday 26 September 2000. With its high ceiling and book-lined walls, the library was an inspired choice of venue for such an occasion. Although the book had already been launched in both London and New York there had been little public awareness of it in Ireland up to that time. For the Dublin event a mass signing was organised, with all the contributors invited to attend from 11 am to 6.00 pm. As they arrived the contributors were given a name-tag and a complimentary copy of the book and were shown by one of the volunteer team of workers to one of twelve large tables placed around the library in alphabetical order. The general public queued to get signatures from their chosen contributors. All the contributors there had given up their day for the cause. Many who weren't used to having their work signed were quite bemused by the whole process. It also became evident as the day wore on that many of the contributors had not met each other before.

The RDS launch must have been one of the biggest mass signings ever to have taken place anywhere and I often wondered if it would get a place in the *Guinness Book of Records*. Most of the contributors sat in their place for the entire day, with just an occasional break. To add to the occasion a four-piece string quartet played on the podium throughout the day. I am sure that a contributing factor to the general atmosphere was that everyone present, whether contributors or the general public, realised that we might need the services of The Irish Hospice Foundation at some stage of our lives. All in all it was a well-organised event and a highly successful launch of the book in Ireland. It would be impossible to estimate the number of people in attendance, as people were coming and going all day. Likewise, I have no idea how many copies of the book were sold on the day, but I heard that one company bought 1000 copies to be distributed among their clients. Other large companies bought consignments to be used as Christmas presents for their employees that year, and a lot of individuals bought copies to send to family and friends living abroad. It was also bought by a number of government departments, including the Department of Foreign Affairs which gave copies to foreign dignitaries. President Mary McAleese used copies as her Christmas gift to her staff that year, and Taoiseach Bertie Ahern presented Bill Clinton with a copy on St Patrick's Day. It was an extraordinary gathering to launch an extraordinary book.

Joe Burgess and I joined the queues at the RDS at around midday on that 26 September. It later emerged that about 175 contributors were present for some or all of the time, and that many of them had travelled from abroad at their own expense. I already had 35 signatures in my copy before the mass signing but with all the comings and goings on the day I couldn't reach as many of the contributors present as I would have liked. Queues varied in size from contributor to contributor, with most people of course lining up for the most famous names. A lot of people had bought multiple copies of the book and naturally wanted all of them signed. This was good for sales but it did slow proceedings down. Despite this, 114 people signed my copy that day, including such notables as Louis Le Brocquy, Guggi, Felim Egan, Patrick Scott, Paul Brady, Gavin Friday, John Rocha, Nell McCafferty, Deirdre Purcell, Frank McGuinness, Marie Heaney, Polly Devlin and Michael Hartnett, as well as committee chairperson Maire Donnelly. Sadly, Michael Hartnett's death was announced two weeks later so this was his last public outing.

Chasing signatures became something of a cult after this and ten years later people still turn up to get their copy of *The Whoseday Book* signed when one of the contributors is launching a book or exhibition. At one stage of the launch proceedings I spotted U2's manager Paul McGuinness entering the library, talking on his mobile phone, so I headed in his direction. He was about to rush off again but he stopped to talk and to sign my book. I asked him if Bono and The Edge were going to put in an appearance at some stage, but he said they were deep in rehearsals for a forthcoming tour. He gave me his card, invited me to write and promised he would get the two of them to sign. Naturally I followed up on his offer the week after and his secretary advised me to send the book along. It was returned quite promptly. The Edge had drawn a smiling face and signed it, while Bono, as well as inscribing the book, drew a large flower and wrote, 'Doc: Make us better – Thanks Pal' Bono.'

Other major pop stars were surprisingly easy to track down over the coming years. Their tours were well advertised in

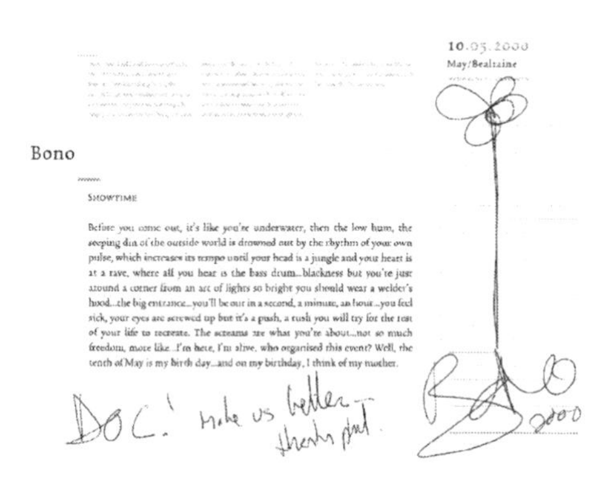

10.05.2000

May/Bealtaine

Bono

SHOWTIME

Before you come out, it's like you're underwater, then the low hum, the seeping din of the outside world is drowned out by the rhythm of your own pulse, which increases its tempo until your head is a jungle and your heart is at a rave, where all you hear is the bass drum...blackness but you're just around a corner from an arc of lights so bright you should wear a welder's hood...the big entrance...you'll be out in a second, a minute, an hour...you feel sick, your eyes are screwed up but it's a push, a rush you will try for the rest of your life to recreate. The screams are what you're about...not so much freedom, more like...I'm here, I'm alive, who organised this event? Well, the tenth of May is my birth day...and on my birthday, I think of my mother.

advance, so on each occasion I contacted the manager of the particular auditorium they were due to play in. I never had a refusal. In this way I got Neil Hannon, Brian Kennedy, Van Morrison, Paddy Maloney, Bob Geldof, Marianne Faithful, Sinéad O'Connor and Ronnie Drew to sign. I had known Ronnie previously and he wrote, 'Of all the Money that ever I spent, I spent it in good company. All the best Philip – Ronnie Drew.'

The Northern Ireland Agreement was being negotiated at this time and it was common knowledge that US Senator George Mitchell was a regular visitor to Ireland. A friend of mine, Brenda McLoughlin, was the Vice-Chancellor of Queen's University, Belfast at the time and had access to Stormont Castle. She took the book to Mr Mitchell on my behalf and, like John Hume before him, he wrote about the peace process, inscribing the page:

For Philip who shares my dream,
Of a durable peace,
Mutual Respect,
And Tolerance in Northern Ireland.
George Mitchell

Mass signings also took place in Cork, in Brown Thomas's in Dublin and in Kenny's Bookshop in Galway, though nothing on the scale of the event in the RDS. Lelia Doolan organised the Galway signing and managed to get 35 contributors to attend. When I went to Kenny's for the day I met many of the contributors who had already signed my copy but I was able to add photographers John Minihan and Fergus Bourke as well as writers Hugh Leonard, Eugene McCabe, Rita Ann Higgins, Tim Robinson and Jennifer Johnston, who wrote 'For a Book-collecting lunatic from Sligo with admiration for your persistence – Jennifer Johnston.' John Minihan was a long-time friend of Bernard Stone and we had a lengthy discussion about him.

Blacklist Section H by Francis Stuart is one of my favourite books and is now regarded as his greatest book. Having corresponded with him some fifteen years earlier I decided to write to him at his Dublin address and ask him to sign my book. He had been dogged by controversy in the early part of his life because of his unwillingness to take a clear moral stand about the years he spent in Nazi Germany. Further controversy was to follow in 1996 when he was elected a Saoi of Aosdána. There were strong objections by some members, with the poet Máire Mhac An tSaoi resigning in protest. I looked at him solely as a writer and felt that he was entitled to his political beliefs. What was past was past. Two weeks after I wrote to him I had a phone call from the artist Finola Graham to tell me that she was Francis's wife and that he had moved from Dublin to her house in Fanore, Co Clare. She also told me that he was in Ennis County Hospital just then, and even though he wasn't in physical distress he was pining for his favourite cat. Knowing of his devotion to cats over the years – I had never seen a photograph of him without a cat in his arms – I said that the presence of his cat at this time would be of far greater benefit to him than whatever medication he was taking. She fully agreed with me. She invited me to send the book to her address in Fanore and promised she would get Francis to sign it. Through my medical contacts I enquired whether he could have his cat with him, even though I knew it would be against hospital policy. He was in a public ward so unfortunately I got the expected answer. Over the next two weeks I spoke to Finola on a few occasions, the last being the morning of Wednesday 2nd January 2000 when she told me that Francis had died the previous night. Fortunately he had been moved to a private room a few days beforehand and I was delighted to hear that he had his cat in his arms when he died. Finola also told me that he had signed my book two nights earlier, which was the last time he held a pen in his hand. He was in his 98th year. I had no idea that he had reached such a great age and I wouldn't have bothered him had I known.

The next day I drove to Fanore to pay my last respects, and as I was unfamiliar with the area I had to ask for directions a few times. On one such occasion I pulled in to the side of the road where two farmers were in deep conversation, standing beside a tractor. When I asked for the road to Fanore, one of them said, 'You see the white line in the middle of the road – shtick to it'. Not another word was said and I continued on my way until I reached the house. On arrival I was met by Finola and her son Liam, Francis's stepson, and was taken to the front room where Francis was laid out in a brown Franciscan habit, with his arms folded across his chest. After I had said a few prayers at the bedside, Finola told me that Francis's cat had just been brought back from the local veterinary office, where it had been put down earlier that morning at her request. She felt that the cat would pine away without Francis so she had decided that it should be buried with him. She asked my opinion about this and when I agreed with what she wanted to do she was delighted. She then asked if I would put the cat in the coffin with him and I said I would be happy to do so.

Francis's son and daughter-in-law were also present in the house and at this stage they all retired to the kitchen, leaving me with Francis and a warm but dead Siamese cat. Rather than hide the cat right under the covers, I put its head in the crook of Francis's left arm just outside the covers – I was very sorry I didn't have a camera. After this I joined the others in the kitchen where a bottle of whiskey was produced and we drank a toast to his memory. My book was then discovered on the back seat of Finola's car, liberally covered with the cat's hairs. Francis's signature was shaky and that of a very old man. A final toast was had before I made my departure. A radio commentator covering the funeral the next day announced that it had become known during the service that Francis's cat had also died and had been buried with him but that the precise cause of the cat's death was a mystery to all.

Obviously my copy of the book was the only one that he signed. He was after all the most senior man of letters in Ireland at the time. Apart from managing to get his signature, the whole saga was quite extraordinary as well as being emotional, and it was something I won't forget. Looking back, this was without doubt the high point of the whole *Whoseday Book* signing for me.

Ex-Taoiseach Charles Haughey's contribution to the book was a reproduction of a Seamus Heaney poem 'The Given Note'. I felt certain that Haughey, with his background as a self-proclaimed man of the arts, would be amenable to my approach so I wrote to him. A few days later my secretary told me that a Mr Haughey wanted to speak to me on the phone. My first thoughts were that someone was having me on, or that the comedian Dermot Morgan had come back to life to haunt me. Even when I took the call and heard the distinctive Haughey voice I still wasn't certain it was him and I knew I could easily put my foot in it. In the event he was charming, talking at length about the book and how pleased he was to be involved in it. He then invited me to his home in Kinsealy where he said he would be happy to sign for me. It was impossible for me to go there at the time so I said I would post the book. He advised against this as he thought the postal system was unsafe, but in the end that is what I did. When it was returned he had inscribed it as follows:

For Philip.
Who's had the great
Fortune to practice the
Noble art of Medicine
Where the Wind
Has bundled up the
Clouds high over
Knocknarea.
Charles Haughey.

Naturally I still regret I didn't take up his invitation. Staying with politicians I next sent the book to Síle De Valera in Dáil Éireann, who also got her Fianna Fáil colleague Charlie McCreevy to sign. Shortly afterwards the book went again to Dáil Éireann, to Liz McManus, who got Ruairi Quinn, then leader of the Labour Party, to sign too. All of this was kept strictly along party lines.

My daughter Jenny was a volunteer helper at the Cúirt in Galway one year, so had ready access to the visiting authors. Naturally I gave her a job to do and during the festival she got writers Brian Keenan, Medbh McGuckian, Aidan Matthews, Colum McCann and Maire Mhac An tSaoi to sign. My son Joe also played his part by taking the book to Thomas Kinsella in Wicklow. Kinsella was about to emigrate to America and I might never have got his signature otherwise. Over the years all three children either delivered the book or collected it on numerous occasions from various contributors. They christened it 'The Bible' and the name has stuck.

In general, the artists involved, in particular the painters Thomas Ryan and Brian Bourke, were creative with their

signing contributions. Thomas Ryan invited me to his studio in Ashbourne, Co Meath, and after he had browsed through the book when I arrived he was very encouraging about what I was attempting to do and said that I was making the best possible use of it. Over the next hour, he painted a watercolour called 'Grattan's Parliament' on his page and wrote 'Will the Stormont one last longer – Thomas Ryan.' Brian Bourke and I arranged to meet in Lee's pub in Moycullen one Saturday afternoon. After a few pints he proceeded to tell me a great story that he said was doing the rounds, about the burial of Francis Stuart and his cat. At first I said nothing and let him finish the story. Then I showed him the relevant signature and told him the unabridged version of the saga. He was highly amused. At that stage he decided to take the book home with him, as he wanted to think about what he would do with his page. When he returned it a few weeks later he had drawn a totally true to life self-portrait. Conor Fallon's original contribution to the book was a drawing of five horses, and on my copy he drew an extra horse, while John Behan drew one of his trade mark bulls on his page. Paul Mosse, Antoine Ó Flatharta, John Stephenson, Paki Smith, Martin McDonagh, Martin Gale and the composers Seoirse Bodley and Brian Boydell all drew images on their respective pages and signed them. Brian Boydell was one of those who hadn't been able to attend the mass signing at the RDS. When I contacted him I was invited to his house, where he told me that it was the first copy he had seen. He was in fact a very sick man, which I hadn't known beforehand, and sadly he died a few months later.

One unusual contribution was from Carlo Gebler, who lives outside Enniskillen. After I made contact with him he invited me to visit whenever I was next passing through. On the day I called he left me browsing the bookshelves in his writer's den while he drew an extensive map that covered his entire page in the book and which outlined in detail the route from Sligo to his house. He is an avid cartographer. Another unusual contribution was from photographer Tony Higgins. He has his own studio in Dublin and is one of the best known of his profession in the country. As well as being the recipient of numerous awards, he has photographed most of our public figures over the years, including politicians, writers, actors, singers and entertainers, and some years ago he did a major photo-shoot for Richard Harris at Harris's home in the Bahamas. On the day I visited Higgins he first looked through the book and then posed the two of us and had his assistant take a photograph. This was pasted onto his page in the book and he duly signed it. I had finally made it into the book myself!

Martyn Turner was easy to make contact with, as he has been contributing political cartoons to *The Irish Times* since 1971 and has published twelve collections of these. After I wrote to him he invited me to send the book on. As well as drawing a wonderful cartoon of 'Bertie the Taoiseach', he inscribed his page as follows: 'Little known facts. Jennifer [referring to Jennifer Johnston on the page opposite] got her entry on her birthday (Which is also the birthday of my wife) … Not many people know that, as Michael Caine might say. Signed in the era of Bertie. Best wishes. Martyn Turner.'

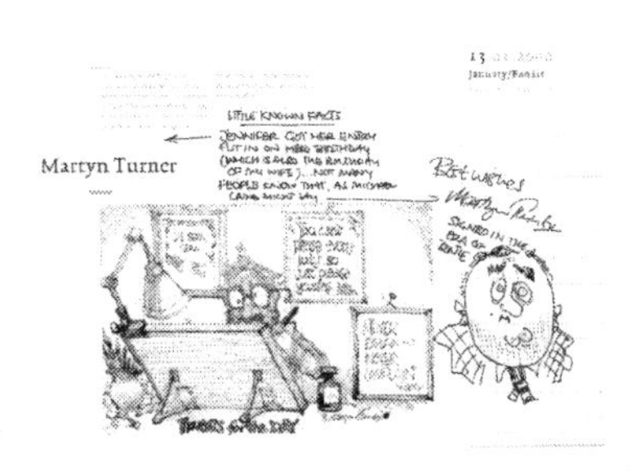

Richard Harris proved very difficult to track down. After a few false starts I discovered that as well as his home in the Bahamas he had a permanent suite in London's Savoy Hotel, where he spent part of the year. When I contacted his secretary, she asked me to send it to her and said she would get him to sign it when he was next in London. He inscribed it 'To Philip. Delighted to join the mob. Richard Harris.' He also drew a smiling face under which he wrote 'Me Happy'. He died some months later.

Michael Longley is a frequent visitor to Sligo and after one of his readings he inscribed it 'For Phil – Lover of books and lover of Sligo – Blessings from Belfast – Michael Longley.' By arrangement I visited the Irish mezzo-soprano Bernadette Greevy in her home in Clontarf one Saturday and she wrote;

These lines explain my life
as a travelling singer
I cannot rest from travel;
I will drink Life to the lees:
All times I have enjoyed greatly,
Have suffered greatly,
Both with those that loved me,
And alone.
Bernadette Greevy

The film-maker Louis Marcus wrote: 'To Philip Murray, I must admire your determination to get us all to sign the book. It will be a unique copy and hope you complete it before some of us end up in The Hospice ourselves! – Louis Marcus.'

After many attempts I tracked down *The Irish Times* meteorologist Brendan McWilliams when he was on a rare visit back to Ireland, and he inscribed the book:'To Philip with best wishes. My apologies that you have had to chase me all over Europe' – Brendan Mc Williams.' By prior arrangement I met the poet Theo Dorgan in Connolly's after a poetry reading and he wrote: 'Here we are in Sligo, Phil, Trying, Trying. Sure what else would we do? To live your life is not so simple as to cross a field. B. L. Pasternak. Here's to the healer – Theo.' On a visit to Dublin I met writer and broadcaster Ferdia Mac Anna by arrangement at the RTÉ Studios in Donnybrook, and he wrote, 'The only rule in life is that there is no rule. Ferdia Mac Anna.' On the same day I visited the poet Robert Greacen at his home in Dublin and he inscribed the book 'For Philip: Delighted to have joined the great and the good who are assembled in this delightful volume – Robert.' He too was another long-time friend and admirer of Bernard Stone and we had a hilarious time recounting tales of Bernard.

The graphic designer Paul O'Connor was someone I hadn't known of previously and when I met him he wrote, 'To Philip Murray. Good detective work! You managed to track me down to a sandwich bar in George's Street Arcade! All the best. Paul O Connor.' Another graphic artist, Robert Armstrong, wrote: 'To Philip. They always talk about the hard won image in painting – Well this is a hard won signature. Robert Armstrong.' The writer Nuala O Faolain, whom I met in her Dublin home, inscribed the book, 'Signed with great pleasure for a man whose response to Irish art and writing has taken the form of an exemplary, persistent quest – who is also the man who interred Francis Stuart's cat with Francis. Nuala O Faolain.'

The general sentiments expressed by those who signed the book were fun-based but singer Christy Moore's was different. His contribution to the book was a song that he had written entitled 'Veronica' and beside it in my book he wrote the following:

> Dear Philip,
> I was out on Cape Clear. I was within hearing range
> Of a radio tuned in to Radio na Gaeltachta.
> There was a newsflash. The only words I
> Recognised were Veronica Guerin. I put 2 and 2
> Together. If Veronica Guerin has been mentioned on
> A newsflash on R Na G there could be only
> One reason and sadly I was right.
> I was so angry and helpless and
> Powerless all I could think to do was write
> A song for this brave foolhardy woman.
> I never met her, but knew about her
> Work and legend.
> I've performed the song right around

The world, and everywhere the people had
Heard of our warrior woman.
Philip I admire you for your
Determination to see this project through and
I hope you catch us all.
Love,
Christy Moore.

The John Huston School of Film and Digital Media was established in University College Galway in 2003 and the official launch took place at the Beverly Hilton in Los Angeles on 2 May that year. About 70 people from Galway went to the event and my friend Tom Kenny told me he could arrange to have the book taken there. The patron of the school, Anjelica Huston, and the Irish-American Merv Griffin, the TV host and owner of the Beverly Hilton, were both contributors and were to attend the launch. John Donnelly, the former drummer with the Saw Doctors band, took my copy of *The Whoseday Book* with him and got both of them sign it. Some time later Tom Kenny again came to the rescue when he got his sister to take it to Jersey, where she lives, for the novelist Jack Higgins to sign. He inscribed it as follows: 'Dear Philip. I'm still writing the bad poetry, still churn out the Dillon books at the restaurant table – a little more difficult at 73 because of essential tremor. New book 'Bad Company'. Trust all is well with you. God Bless. – Jack Higgins.'

On more than one occasion a contributor would get someone else they knew to sign my copy before returning it in the post. Or sometimes they would give me phone numbers or addresses of people who hadn't yet signed. Some even sent back the return postage I had enclosed. June Levine got her husband, psychiatrist Ivor Brown, to sign as well as their near neighbour, playwright Tom Murphy. June wrote 'Dear Philip – Thank heavens for crazy endeavour – so often more creative than sanity. June Levine.' The painter Barrie Cooke had signed my book at an earlier stage but one Christmas when he was visiting Kilkenny, where he had previously lived, he took my copy with him and got fellow artists Tony O'Malley, Sonja Landweer and Hughie O'Donoghue to sign it.

Another graphic artist I had difficulty locating was Alan

Aboud. He lives in London and travels the world with his work. Through a mutual friend I finally made contact with his mother in Dublin, who undertook to have him sign on his next visit to Ireland. When he did so he also got his two young sons, Victor and Milo, to sign on the same page – they are certainly starting young! After the book was returned I wrote to Alan to thank him and tell him that Francis Stuart was the oldest to have signed and his two boys were the youngest.

The person to have signed most recently is Tom Hayden, the American social and political activist. Apart from being of Irish descent he is most famous for his involvement in the anti-war and civil rights movements of the sixties and for having been married to Jane Fonda. On his page he wrote: 'See the eyes of the Belfast girl, and take them into all our hearts. – Tom Hayden.' (He was referring to a Belfast girl who appeared in the photograph on his page.) I sent the book to him in Los Angeles and the round trip took two weeks.

In all, the copy was in the post on 84 occasions, once to America, fifteen times to England, and 68 times within the island of Ireland, so again I must compliment the postal systems around the world. My friends and family advised me time and again to stop sending it in the post as it was too risky, but I continued to take chances. My main worry was that the copy would get into the hands of some unscrupulous person who would tear out the page of someone very famous and thereby render the book incomplete. There was only one major hiccup: I sent the copy to the historian Marianne Elliott in Liverpool and she was about to return it when there was a lightning postal strike, so she had to have it sent back by courier. A few years ago I wrote to the chief executive of An Post to tell of my good news story and to compliment his organisation on the level of service I had experienced. I had a very grateful reply. Despite all the travelling it has done, the book is in remarkably good condition, most of which I would attribute to the presence of its sturdy slip case, in which it travelled at all times.

So far in this odyssey 354 contributors have either signed or inscribed for me, far more than I had hoped for originally. They include the famous and the not so famous and I have had the pleasure of meeting about 200 of them. Over this time, whether I made contact by letter or by phone, I didn't have a single refusal. As well as the stories told in the preceding pages, there are many more to tell about the rest of those who signed, and particularly about how I managed to track them down. My copy has been signed in all sorts of places – people's homes, pubs, libraries, hotels, restaurants, in or on cars, at readings and book launches, and in my own house. Everyone who signed it was very encouraging about what I was doing, though of course there were also those who thought I was a little mad. Perhaps they were right.

A common theme among the contributors was the genuine delight they showed at being in the book. Many wanted to talk or write about the reason for their own contribution, which in some instances was to do with personal bereavements. What became increasingly obvious as time went on was that more and more people wanted to write or draw on their page rather than just sign it. This usually occurred after they had looked through my copy and seen what others had contributed. Something else that became apparent was that many people used their personal copy of the book as an actual diary, or in some instances as a visitors' book. One hairdresser used it as an appointments book, and one well-known restaurant printed their daily menu on the appropriate page throughout that year.

At the outset I decided I was going to leave the book to my elder daughter Emily, to be kept as a family heirloom, and that is what will happen. When I mentioned this to some of the contributors they inscribed the book to both Emily and myself. If I have a regret, it is that I didn't have a second copy with me to get the contributors I met in person to sign rather than inscribe it. I could then have given that copy to The Irish Hospice Foundation so that they could put it up for auction. Unfortunately the thought struck me when it was too late to do this. However, *The Whoseday Book* raised over €3 million which must make it one of the most successful fund-raising events undertaken in Ireland. Two similar schemes were undertaken in the following two years. *Art: Pack in 2001* was a set of playing cards with each card designed by an artist. *Peter and the Wolf* in 2002 was an ambitious project that included a full-colour book illustrated by U2's Bono and his daughter and a CD narrated by the singer

Gavin Friday, with the music performed by the Gavin Friday/ Maurice Seezer Ensemble. Though successful, neither this nor the *Art: Pack* venture raised anything like *The Whoseday Book* undertaking.

It is fascinating now to look back on the ten years since the book was launched. For me the project I undertook has been a huge success, as never in my wildest dreams did I envisage getting so many signatures. About 35 of the original 366 contributors are now dead. (My friend Peter Fallon, who had helped me with a few signatures, wrote to me some time ago and said 'Isn't it very annoying when some people haven't the manners not to die before they have signed.') Those who are still alive but haven't signed my book include singer Enya, writers Simon Reilly, Marsha Hunt, Bridget O'Connor, Mary Higgins Clark and Robert Bernen, as well as architect Kevin Roche. I haven't entirely given up but I feel the project has run its course.

Epilogue

Now that I have finally finished this book I must look back and try to answer some questions, such as 'What have I learnt?' 'What is book-collecting?' and 'What has it meant to me?'

Even though I have made only a brief foray into the business I have certainly learnt a little about the life of a professional writer. One thing that strikes me is that it can be a very lonely and difficult life. When John Braine signed my copy of *Room at the Top* in 1983 he wrote, 'Thank you very much for your appreciation of my work. I very much depend upon my readers, and a letter like yours is very encouraging, since writing is essentially a lonely job. I'll be delighted to sign your copy. Sincerely. John Braine.' A Benedictine monk, Brother Rougeau, is reported as saying, 'Monks and writers lead very similar lives. We spend our best time in retreat from the world, anxious to make something of our rich experience. What is difficult is receiving any sort of public attention' (Doreen Carvajal, *New York Times*, Books section, 19 June 2001). There are writers all over the world trying to break through and get published and many must be in great despair about the number of rejected manuscripts littering their floors. Many famous authors in later life speak about the misery they experienced taking a manuscript from publisher to publisher, getting one rejection after another and sometimes knowing that the manuscript wasn't even read. On top of that, there are so many of us who think we have the great novel just waiting to get out, which of course rarely happens.

The saddest thing that has happened in my 35 years as a collector is the huge decline in the number of bookshops. George Bernard Shaw said in 1909, 'What we want above all things is not more books, not more publishers, not more education, not more literary genius, but simply and prosaically more shops.' The same thing has happened to bookshops as happened to old-fashioned grocery stores when supermarkets came along. The decline in the number of shops has also meant a decline in the number of wonderful characters who owned these establishments. They have been replaced in many, though not all, instances by shop assistants whose knowledge of books is, to say the least, limited.

Modern bookshops also stock fewer examples of serious literature, because such books take up valuable shelf space without showing the necessary financial return. Blockbusters, where the money is, must be promoted heavily and given the most space. And in true supermarket fashion the new bookshop chains sell two books for the price of one, or three for the price of two, making it hard for the small bookseller to compete.

Another unfortunate trend is that so many of the better books get stolen that many bookshops now need security cameras. The most celebrated case of book theft concerned one Stephen Blumberg, who in 1991 was sentenced to nearly six years in jail for stealing 23,000 books from various bookshops and libraries all over North America. Apparently he had good taste and only went for the best, building up a major library of valuable books. Interestingly, when the police tried to return these books to their rightful homes many of the libraries and institutions whose property they were hadn't realised they were missing.

Technology has also played a negative part by killing an element of the chase, which is one of the fundamentals of book-collecting. In the past, one could wait three or four years to get a sighting of a scarce book, and sometimes perhaps it would never appear. But now all that needs to be done is to go on the internet and probably find that numerous copies are available. Technology must make things easier for dealers, of course, as they can easily check the price of any book they may be unsure about. As a result, many dealers worldwide only trade in the upper and rarer end of the market. What this will do for publishing and book collecting has yet to emerge.

In my book-collecting life I have hardly ever paid more than the published price for a book, and in many instances I paid a lot less because I found them secondhand or remaindered. As well as my four principal author collections — Patrick White, Liam

O'Flaherty, Seamus Heaney and Cormac McCarthy — I have collected many other authors without trying to acquire their secondary material. None of my collections is absolutely complete in the strict sense, and each has presented a different challenge along the way.

We have been told many times over the years that the whole future of the publishing industry is in doubt and that the demise of the book as we know it is imminent, again because of advances in technology. There may be some truth in this rumour and I am somewhat pessimistic about the whole thing. The market in e-books is growing and we can now get them downloaded to our laptops at the press of a button. The cost of books bought in this way is a fraction of that of hard copies so it is financially attractive. Computer-literate young people are more likely to go down this road than those in my age group. It is depressing to think that in the future an entire book collection might be contained in a laptop, making the title of Anthony Powell's book *Books do Furnish a Room* no longer accurate. Also, getting books signed will become a thing of the past. The only saving grace with this technology is that a library of books can be carried so easily on holiday or travelling for other reasons.

It is also worrying that seismic changes are taking place in the newspaper industry around the world, leading some commentators to forecast that the industry is in terminal decline. In America alone more than 150 newspapers closed down in 2010 and some of the main players are in serious trouble. I hope this is not a sign of things to come for the book industry.

Writing this book has been a worthwhile exercise for me. Even though it hasn't all been plain sailing, I am glad I did it — life would have been that much duller if I hadn't. At one stage I took a complete break from writing for two months and very nearly didn't come back to it. One of my biggest problems concerned autobiographical material, so I decided to omit everything to do with medicine, sport and personal issues and to list only the main landmarks in my life. Another difficulty I identified early on was that of name-dropping. When I mentioned this to Des Kenny he said that to write such a book it was necessary to name-drop, and that this was totally acceptable where it was relevant. The book has taken me over two and a half years to complete, during which I wrote five drafts by hand before committing the text to a more legible form with my one-finger typing. Then there were repeated corrections, additions and deletions, all of which led to further drafts. This project has certainly taught me the difference between reading a book and writing one, and I can empathise with what Jorge Luis Borges said in *The Craft of Verse* on the subject of reading: 'I think the happiness of a reader is beyond that of a writer, for a reader need feel no trouble, no anxiety: he is merely out for happiness. And happiness, when you are a reader, is frequent.'

In every sense writing this account of my book-collecting life has been a trip down memory lane and a great period of reflection for me. I can recommend the process to anyone. As I said in the prologue, I set out with a spirit of adventure, though naturally there were times when I wondered what I was doing, and why, and came seriously close to throwing all the pages in the bin. But book-collecting had been a hobby for me for a long time and I am sure my enthusiasm for it kept me going.

Reading for me is one of life's great pleasures and I now know that life would have been much poorer without it. These days I find myself more and more often rereading old favourites from either my own shelves or from the library. The old dictum 'If it is worth reading, it is worth rereading' still rings true. When I started collecting books I wasn't to know that it would turn into a lifetime pursuit and would give me such pleasure in both reading some great books and making many valued friendships. At this stage I can count as friends a lot of people I have met through books, including fellow readers and collectors, dealers, and writers. In particular I must mention my guru, Bernard Stone – the ultimate book man. It is now obvious to me that when I set out to get *Soft Day*, the Turret Broadsides, *The Whoseday Book* and much else signed by all the contributors it was a direct result of Bernard's influence — how else can I explain this madness?

Acknowledgements

There are many people I want to thank for their assistance and friendship along the way: Des Kenny for planting the seed and for his advice and criticism; Currach Press, my publisher; the late Bernard Stone for everything; Jim O Halloran; Conor Kenny; my fellow collectors Des Lally, Pat Brennan and Kevin Whelan; Maeve O Connor for surgery on my prose and punctuation; Peter Fallon; poets Hugo Williams, Adrian Mitchell, K. T. Canning, Brian Patten, Seamus Heaney, Susan Barker, and Lawrence Ferlinghetti for their contributions; Tom Kenny; Dermot Healy for his introduction and advice; Seamus Cashman; the many writers and artists who gave their time so generously; photographers Chris Felver, Karl Brennan, Dallan Healy, Vivien Murray, Alberto Darszon, Jenny Murray and Dean Kiely; my friends and fellow readers, who unknowingly had an input; and many others too numerous to mention.

My main thanks go to my wife Vivien and my three children, Emily, Joe and Jenny, who gave me great support right from the time I announced that I was going to try to write a book. They probably thought that I was about to vegetate and that this would be a good form of occupational therapy. Over the years they each played a part in my book collecting and put up with my quirks along the way. The three great passions in my life have been Vivien, rugby and book-collecting (note that I have been very careful about the order in which these are listed).

Any profits from the sale of this book will go to The Irish Hospice Foundation.